£ILL - 95p

D0506142

Chapel Tower from Meads   (*Transparency: John Durran*)

First Published September, 1981
Second Edition, February 1989
ISBN 0-900796-03-0

WINCHESTER COLLEGE

After 606 Years, 1382-1988

By
JAMES SABBEN-CLARE

©

J S-C

Published by P. & G. WELLS,
College Street, Winchester

Printed by Brown & Son (Ringwood) Ltd.,
Crowe Arch Lane, Ringwood.

Nine Old Wykehamist Judges at the Ad Portas ceremony, 1981.
(Photograph: E.A. Sollars)

FOREWORD TO FIRST EDITION

By

The Rt.Hon. the Lord Aldington, P.C., K.C.M.G., C.B.E., D.S.O., T.D., M.A.
(Warden, Winchester College)

This book presents the story of Winchester College in its sixth centenary, paying particular attention to the last 150 years. It shows in a manner worthy of a dedicated Winchester scholar, who is now Second Master, how our fourteenth century Foundation has adapted to political, ideological and social movements in our national life during recent decades. The story has not been told before, because it could not be.

The history of Winchester College written by the much loved Budge Firth in 1949 sought to relate our College to outside conditions over its long history. Thirty-two years later we can see more clearly how great the changes in those outside conditions have been during this century and where the conditions of life and learning at Winchester are different from those in earlier days, and where they are similar.

How many other changes will be brought by the next few decades and how earlier traditions may be carried forward, the reader may like to ponder — as do my colleagues and myself. For the life stream of Winchester College education flows on down the valley of the changing years, always drawing strength from William of Wykeham's source and from the tributaries that it meets during the years.

The Warden (Sir Jeremy Morse) and the Headmaster (James Sabben-Clare)
Photograph: E.A. Sollars

CONTENTS

Aerial picture of College   *(Photograph: Aerofilms)*

List of Illustrations

*The back of School being used for bat-fives, with Cloisters and Chapel Tower.
Print of c.1850*

PREFACE TO FIRST EDITION

There are in existence quite a number of books on the history of Winchester College, but none as yet takes the story beyond the Second World War, and so thoroughly has the face of the Public Schools changed in the last thirty-five years that a new appraisal needs little further justification. Even so a bit more time might have been allowed to elapse, to lengthen the perspective, but for the imminence of the school's six hundredth anniversary, an event which encourages reflection and mental stock-taking. 1982 is the date, and that in itself may seem strange to those who recall that the Quingentenary was celebrated in 1893. Wykehamical perversity is not unknown, but does that — or an overdose of inflation — explain how a century can have shrunk to 89 years? The explanation is more mundane. 1382 was the year when William of Wykeham published his Foundation Charter, and 1394 when members of the school first occupied the buildings. It was this latter event that was commemorated in 1893. Unfortunately an early Fellow of the College, who wrote a life of Wykeham in 1424, gave the date of the Opening Day as 1393, and the error was not detected until it was just too late to save the blushes of the organisers of the five hundredth anniversary.

If 1982 provides the occasion for this book, the production of it would not have been possible without the initial encouragement and subsequent support of the Warden and Fellows who gave me free access to the College archives. I am particularly indebted to the present Warden, Lord Aldington, for his personal involvement in the project. Of my colleagues on the teaching staff, I owe most to the Headmaster John Thorn, and to two Archivists past and present, Peter Gwyn and Roger Custance; but there are many others, too numerous to mention by name, whose help I would like to acknowledge for discussion of individual points that have arisen in the course of writing. I have also learnt much from the many Old Wykehamists, not least my father, with whom I have talked and corresponded.

In the course of the past decade several boys in the school have assisted me in looking after the Wiccamica Collection of archives, and so helped to provide the material for this book; I would like particularly to thank Jonathan Bracken and, for their help with the photographs, Andrew Spokes and Timothy Wilson. Nearly all the illustrations come from the school's own collection, and acknowledgement is made wherever the original provenance is known. Some others have been specially provided by my colleagues John Durran and Richard Shorter, and also by Bob Sollars who deserves particular mention for his rich contribution to the pictorial archives of the College and City during the past quarter-century.

The text is intended to be self-explanatory, and the peculiarities of the Winchester language or "notions" have been largely excluded. Where, for convenience, such words do occur, the meaning should not be too hard to identify (e.g. *div* for class, *dons* for masters, *Collegemen* for scholars). But it may be helpful to know that a boy is *up to books* when he is at his lessons, and does his evening preparation in *toytime;* also that the school's joint Head Boys are the Prefect of Hall (a scholar, the senior of the five "Officers" who have particular areas of responsibility) and the Senior Commoner Prefect. One feature of the language is that with certain names such as Chapel and Hall the definite article is usually omitted. So when the word "College" is used on its own it refers to the scholars as a body or to the original buildings where they live, and similarly "School" means the 17th century school-room. Some more exotic terminology may be found in Chapter VIII. Annotations have been limited to some Bibliographical Notes at the end, but for those who wish to verify that I have verified my references, I have deposited in the College archives a manuscript copy with a full quota of footnotes.

Finally I wish to thank Jo Lloyd for her invaluable secretarial help, and my wife and family for support and forbearance given in equally generous measures. But all this would have been for nothing without the courtesy and cooperation of my publisher, Paul Cave, who so readily accepted this book as the third in his Winchester trilogy.

PREFACE TO SECOND EDITION

Many Wykehamists have been kind enough to write to me about this book in the seven years since it was published. The oldest of the correspondents, Major A.L. Ashwell, was 95 when he wrote, having come to the school in 1899. Others spanned nearly every subsequent generation. Between them they have considerably enlarged my understanding of a number of things in the school's history, as well as politely correcting a few errors in the text. A second edition gives me an opportunity to put those things right as well as bringing the information up to date.

For the opportunity to undertake this revision I owe a deep debt of gratitude to Al Gordon of New York whose generosity is matched by two things only: his love of Trollope, and of Trollope's one time school — Winchester College.

James Sabben-Clare

Middle Gate reflected in the door of Chapel.

(Transparency: John Durran)

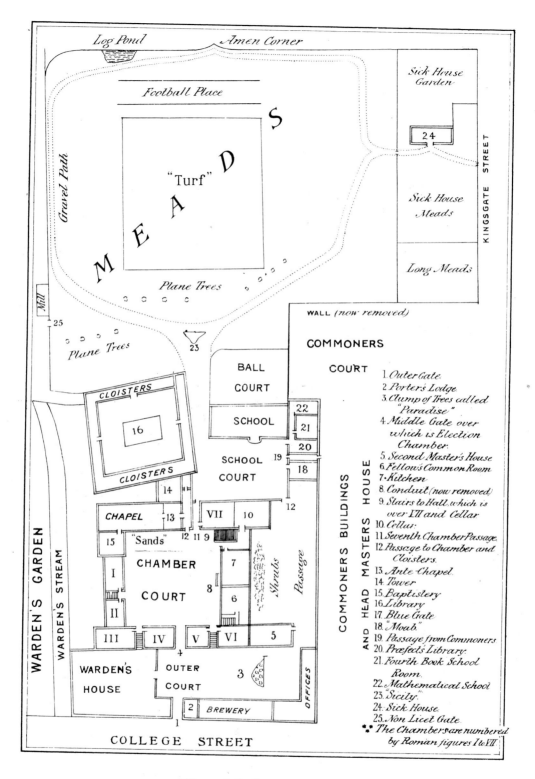

Log Pond   Amen Corner

Sick House Garden

Football Place

M E A D S

"Turf"

24

Gravel Path

KINGSGATE STREET

Sick House Meads

Mill

Plane Trees

Long Meads

25

Plane Trees

23

WALL (now removed)

COMMONERS

COURT

BALL COURT

SCHOOL

CLOISTERS

22

21

16

20

19

18

CLOISTERS

SCHOOL COURT

14

12

CHAPEL

13

VII

10

15

"Sands"

12 11 9

WARDEN'S GARDEN

CHAMBER

7

WARDEN'S STREAM

I

8

6

Shrubs

Passage

COMMONERS BUILDINGS AND HEAD MASTERS HOUSE

COURT

II

III

IV

V

VI

5

WARDEN'S

OUTER

3

HOUSE

COURT

4

OFFICES

2   BREWERY

1

COLLEGE   STREET

1. Outer Gate.
2. Porter's Lodge.
3. Clump of Trees called "Paradise".
4. Middle Gate over which is Election Chamber.
5. Second Master's House.
6. Fellow's Common Room.
7. Kitchen.
8. Conduit (now removed).
9. Stairs to Hall, which is over VII and Cellar.
10. Cellar.
11. Seventh Chamber Passage.
12. Passage to Chamber and Cloisters.
13. Ante-Chapel.
14. Tower.
15. Baptistery.
16. Library.
17. Blue Gate.
18. "Moab".
19. Passage from Commoners.
20. Præfect's Library.
21. Fourth Book School Room.
22. Mathematical School.
23. "Sicily".
24. Sick House.
25. Non Licet Gate.
. The Chambers are numbered by Roman figures I to VII.

Plan of College, 1835-40

xiv

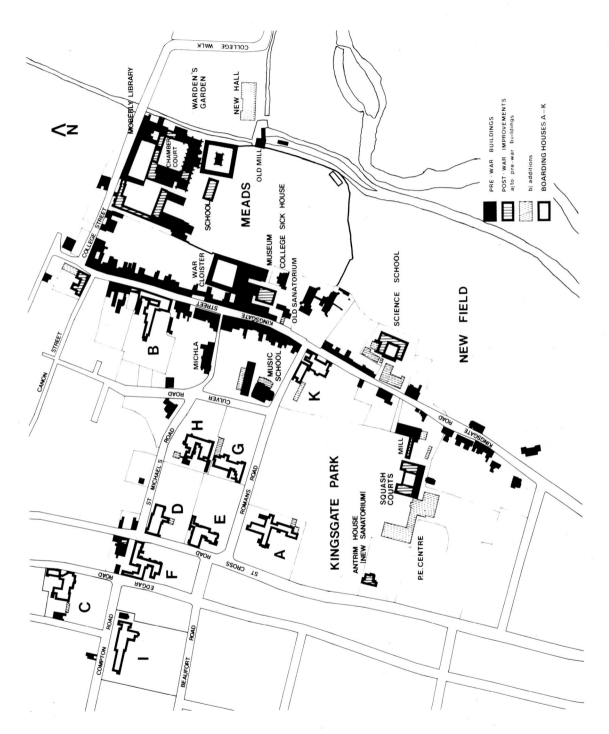

Plan of College in 1982

The founder with the Virgin Mary. (*Transparency: John Durran*)

Chapter I

Six Hundred Years

"Richard by the grace of God King of England and France and Lord of Ireland to all those whom this letter reaches, greeting. Know that of our special grace and upon the supplication of the reverend father in Christ William of Wykeham Bishop of Winchester we have granted and given licence on behalf of ourselves and our heirs, so far as is in our power, that our beloved in Christ the Prior and Convent of St. Swithun's Winchester may be able to give to the said Bishop one plot of one and a half acres of land and three acres of meadow with its appurtenances in the Soke of Winchester beside the city of Winchester . . . to be had and held by the same Bishop and his successors of us and our heirs for ever . . . and that the said Bishop may be able to found a College or House or Hall to the honour and glory of God and of the glorious Virgin Mary His Mother and to the increase of divine service . . . and to assign and attribute a definite name to this same College or House or Hall, and therein to place and establish a Warden and poor scholars to the number of sixty and ten, studying in grammar according to the wishes of the aforesaid Bishop."

6 October, sixth year of Richard II (1382)

The Royal Licence from which this translated extract comes gave William of Wykeham the final permission he needed to found his College at Winchester. The idea had already been years in germination, perhaps since 1369 when he started to buy land in Oxford, or at any rate since 1373 when he made an agreement with Master Richard of Herton that he should undertake to teach grammar to a group of boys maintained at the Bishop's cost. The purchases at Oxford led to the building of New College whose foundation stone was laid on 5 March 1380, and it was to guarantee for this institution a constant supply of pupils well grounded in Latin that he undertook the construction of a proper school at Winchester.

In 1378 he had obtained a Papal Bull which allowed him to appropriate Downton Rectory in the diocese of Salisbury for the support and maintenance of his intended scholars. He had then to find land on which to build. This apparently occasioned him much less difficulty than he found in Oxford where only the ravages of the Black Death which had left the area by the city walls "full of filth, dirt, and stinking carcasses" enabled him after ten years to complete the necessary purchases.

At Winchester the five-acre site in the Soke, just outside the city walls, was mostly the property of the Benedictine Priory of St. Swithun. Between this and College Street stood two private houses belonging to Thomas Tanner and Thomas Lavington, which Wykeham purchased, and three belonging to the See of Winchester, which he was allowed to annexe. The contracts of sale were drawn up within a week of the issue of the Royal Licence, and a week later on 20 October Wykeham published his Foundation Charter which contains a clear expression, more eloquent in Latin than in English, of his purposes:

"As experience which instructs us in all things makes clear, Grammar is without doubt the foundation gateway and mainspring of all the liberal arts and without it arts of this kind cannot be known nor will anyone be able to attain to the pursuit of them: considering furthermore that through the knowledge of Letters justice is cherished and the prosperity of the human condition is advanced and that some students of other sciences through lack of good learning and sufficient facility in Grammar often fall into the danger of failure when they have given up their enthusiasm for progress. There are also and will be in the future, one may believe, many poor scholars engaged in scholastic disciplines who, suffering from indigence and shortage of money, lack and will lack in the future the means for continuing and advancing in the aforesaid art of Grammar; and so that the poor and needy scholars of this kind, present and future, may be able to devote more time and leisure to the study of Letters and by the grace of God become more richly and freely proficient in mastery and knowledge of Grammar and may become, as is meet, more fitted for the liberal arts and sciences, to enlarge the name of all the arts and sciences and to increase the number of students and masters of those same subjects, so far as in our power, we propose out of our resources and goods conferred upon us by God and with the assistance of divine mercy to set our hands to help and bestow our charity to support them."

The work of the school began at once, although it was not until 28 March 1394 that the College was opened and the scholars could move into their new quarters. It is a quite remarkable thing that nearly six hundred years later most of the original buildings should still be standing, and within and around them the process of education should still be carried on by

Outer Gate, looking towards College Street, completed in 1397.
Engraving by C.W. Radclyffe (1846).

the same people as are named in the original statutes — albeit in different ways and in company with many others: a Warden and ten Fellows, two masters, seventy scholars, three chaplains, three lay-clerks, and sixteen quiristers or choirboys.

Such continuity, unique among schools and rivalled by few other institutions of any kind, has only been made possible by the tenacity with which the College authorities have protected its and their own interests, by the way in which they have responded to the pressure for reform, and not least by the operation of chance.

The closest that the school has yet come to extinction was at the time of the English Reformation. By the Act of 1534 Henry VIII had made himself Supreme Head of the Church in England and thus entitled to the tithes and first-fruits which had previously gone to the Pope. To discover what these revenues might amount to a valuation was undertaken of all ecclesiastical properties. For this purpose Thomas Cromwell, the King's Vicar-General, and his Commissioner Dr. Lee paid a visit to the College in the spring of 1535. The Warden and Fellows did not go out of their way to provide lavish entertainment, and the limit of their generosity was the gift of an old patched-up salt cellar. Maybe they would have tried a bit harder to win Master Cromwell's favour were it not that the King himself happened to be staying at Wolvesey Palace over the road and was able to accept two oxen, ten sheep, and twelve capons "for his favours in matters concerning the College." The nature of the "favours" was shown in the Act of 1536 which exempted from the payment of dues not only the Universities of Oxford and Cambridge, but also the Colleges of Winchester and Eton, "where youth and good wits be educate and nourished in virtue and learning". Henry, representing himself as patron of the liberal arts and sciences, did not wish such pupils to be discouraged and to "give their minds to such other things and fantasies as should neither be acceptable to God nor profitable for his public wealth."

So when the Act of Suppression came into force in 1539, Winchester profited not only by its own exemption, but also by being able to purchase — through the mediation of its own Steward who did extremely well out of the deal — the College of St. Elizabeth which lay adjacent to the school grounds on the eastern side.The original idea was to use this to provide more teaching room, but harsher counsels prevailed and the buildings were demolished to provide stone for the construction of a new wall around Meads.

Saved from the worst of Henry's assaults on religious houses, Winchester seemed only to have won a temporary reprieve. For a Chantries Act in 1546 specifically included Colleges which had been exempted ten years earlier. A second valuation revealed a truer picture of the school's wealth, with the annual income assessed at £947 compared to £700 in 1535. It is difficult to believe that the King could have resisted adding this precious jewel to

College Sick House, or Bethesda, built by Warden John Harris in 1656-7. Engraving by C.W. Radclyffe (1846).

his collection had not death stayed his rapacious hand on 28 January 1547.

Although this stroke of providence removed the immediate danger of dissolution, the Reformation also destroyed the original reason for the school's existence, namely the maintenance of an educated priesthood. An Act passed in the first year of Edward VI's reign for converting Chantries and Colleges to "good and godly uses" made it clear that from then on the religious function of the school was to be subordinated entirely to the educational one. To Winchester this made little difference except that the Fellows, having lost their liturgical duties, had little left to do in the College and less reason for living there. However the fact that they continued to divide among themselves the surplus revenues provided the strongest possible inducement to keep the College going. So long as they observed their statutory obligations to the scholars, which meant among other things being very careful to avoid extravagance in the matter of their daily rations, it was reasonable to suppose that no one would examine their methods of management too closely.

This concern for their own pockets and persons helps to explain the extreme caution of the political attitudes adopted by successive Wardens: though there were a number of Old Wykehamists whose stubbornness or heterodoxy led to disgrace, imprisonment, or even the martyr's stake, the school itself was never involved. The Civil War brought fighting and looting to the streets of Winchester, but thanks to the supreme diplomacy of Warden Harris (1630-1658), the College buildings survived unscathed, with the help of Wykehamists like Nicholas Love, M.P. for Winchester, and Col. Nathaniel Fiennes who lodged in College the night before Parliamentarian troops pillaged the rest of the town in December 1642. Warden Harris survived the scrutiny of a Parliamentary Committee of Religion in 1649 and lived to see the school enriched in the following decade by a large gift of manuscripts from the Government and by the first substantial addition to the College buildings since the 15th century — a Sick House for the scholars. His policy of discretion and self-effacement was a lesson to all who held that office during the times of trouble. He wrote to a friend (in Latin): "I restrain myself and I recommend such restraint to you and all my friends; nothing is more important at this juncture. There is enough fighting and quarrelling all about us, and we should fight and strive for peace with all our powers."

Thus by sedulous attention to their own advantage the Warden and Fellows did their best to ensure the prosperity of the school. There were occasional attacks on the liberties they were taking, but the frequency of the episcopal Scrutinies and Visitations between, for instance, 1605 and 1640 is itself an indication of the futility of the Injunctions that usually followed: there was quite simply no power to enforce them. There is no sign of disquiet in the minds of those who enjoyed this life of ease until the Wardenship of Henry Bigg (1730-40). In a series of papers he tried to persuaded the Fellows of the need to consider their obligations as commensurate with their privileges: we are not absolute proprietors but trustees, he said, yet we do not provide for other members of the College in a just and equitable proportion; we allow to our private uses sums of money which we have no warrant for so allotting; if we cannot justify our present conduct, let us resolve as honest men so to regulate our practice for the future that we may be able to keep a conscience void of offence towards God and towards man.

But statements of high principle, lacking even the example of self-denial on the part of the speaker, could not hope to effect any change, and would not succeed until the liberal conscience had armed itself with the panoply of Law. This first seemed likely to happen in 1818 when the Brougham Commission of Inquiry into the Abuse of Charities connected with the Education of the Poor, heedless of the affront caused by including the venerable establishments of Eton and Winchester within its purview, remarked on the "considerable deviations" made from the original plans of the founders, deviations "dictated more by a regard to the interests of the Fellows than of the scholars" and suggested that the number of scholars might be increased to make proper use of the increased revenues. Bridling with self-righteousness, the Fellows replied with an ingenuous *tu quoque* to the effect that the founder had fixed the number at seventy and it would be quite wrong to deviate from his Charter. The strength of conservative opinion in those pre-Reform days was in any case strong enough to prevent this disagreeable investigation being taken any further, and when the cold eye of a Royal Commission was finally turned on the Public Schools themselves in 1861-2, the forces of change had already begun to assert themselves from within.

The nature of those changes, brought about during the last century and a half, forms the subject of this book. In 1830 the school was little different from its mediaeval self except that there was more accommodation for Commoners, more organized games, and fewer trappings of the religious life. It was completely centralized and occupied little more than its original site; the bounds were so restrictive that no boy was allowed into College Street or Kingsgate Street, and Commoners were debarred even from Meads; the monastic harshness of life had been so little softened that boys were still required to rise at 5.30 a.m. with no prospect of breakfast (bread and beer) until 10; the teaching was all done in one room by a tiny handful of masters and concentrated very largely on Latin; in one respect it was even worse, since the prefects had arrogated new powers to themselves which made callous exploitation and brutality an inevitable part of school-life. In 1988 the school occupies a substantial part of the south-east quarter of the city of Winchester; the eleven housemasters have a considerable measure of independence; boys travel freely to London or further on their free afternoons; many have their own studies and enjoy a standard of living unimaginable even thirty years ago; a staff more numerous than the boys themselves were at the foundation teaches a remarkably wide range of subjects with technological aids of ever-increasing sophistication; there is space, equipment, and expert instruction for a rich variety of games, arts, and recreations; and pervading everything is an ethos of liberal humanism which makes the welfare of every individual a matter of equal importance.

Some of this transformation has been imposed by external factors — Acts of Parliament governing the management and working conditions of the school and so on — but more has been brought about spontaneously by the school's sensitivity to changing attitudes and expectations among that section of the public which provides its clientele. The man who bears the greatest responsibility for assessing the different forces at work, and for keeping in balance the conflicting claims of tradition and innovation, is the Headmaster. Since the powers of the Warden and Fellows were curtailed by the Public Schools Act of 1868, he has had control over matters of internal policy, but even before that he was able to take the initiative in shedding some of the dead weight of mediaeval practice.

Ten Headmasters have contributed to the process described from different points of view in subsequent chapters, and it may be found convenient to have their names set out in order beforehand.

George Moberly (1836-66) was, like all the other Headmasters of the 19th century, himself a Wykehamist, though he had made little mark during his schooldays. A man of keen intellect and the highest principles, believing steadfastly in the educational virtues of Classics and Christian doctrine, he viewed the movement towards reform with an amused tolerance, and emerged with his dignity unscathed by the probings of the Clarendon Commission in 1862. Though suspicious of innovation, he was magnanimous enough to acknowledge that his suspicions were sometimes ill-founded. Without his preparatory work the changes effected by his successor would have been impossible to achieve in so short a time.

George Ridding (1867-84), himself a former scholar and Second Master as his father had been before him, was appointed by invitation of a Governing Body that was still hopeful of preserving its ancient prerogatives. But their privileges were swept away by Parliament, and Ridding showed that he was no great respecter of tradition either by initiating, mostly at his own expense, such change and expansion as earned him the title of Second Founder. As a person he was difficult to get alongside, being by nature unsociable and further embittered by the early death of his first wife, a daughter of George Moberly. His relations with both masters and boys suffered as a consequence, and the great material benefits that he conferred on the school were to some extent offset by the public humiliation which he brought on himself by his handling of the Tunding Row of 1872 (see p.44).

William Andrewes Fearon (1884-1901), nicknamed The Bear, was a totally dedicated Wykehamist: apart from two years as Headmaster of Durham School he spent almost all of his very long life as a member of one of Wykeham's communities. He was one of only two applicants for Ridding's post and was appointed without interview. His upbringing inclined him to be traditionalist in his thinking, and he had little new to offer as Headmaster. His virtues — abundant energy and wide interests — were seen to their best advantage in his teaching and housemastering, but at least his geniality made the Headmaster's position less remote and awe-inspiring than it had been before.

Hubert Murray Burge (1901-1911) was the first Headmaster to be appointed in open competition — there were twelve other candidates — and was also a non-Wykehamist. He accepted the post even though he had

George Ridding, Headmaster 1867-1884. A 'Spy' cartoon from Vanity Fair made in 1901 when Ridding was Bishop of Southwell.

completed less than a year as Headmaster of Repton. It is as well for Winchester that he did so, since he deserves to be ranked among the best of the school's Headmasters, in spite of his name not being widely known. He did more than anyone else to modernize the curriculum and raise the status of artistic education, acting on the revolutionary principle "that it was necessary to adapt a boy's education to his character and ability" rather than force him into a mould. Science Building and Music School stand as his permanent memorials. A man of great personal charm with an enviable knack of remembering names and faces, he was always a sympathetic listener even on occasions where he had already made up his own mind. He also had that gift most essential to all Headmasters, the ability to pick people of outstanding quality for his staff.

The name Montague John Rendall (1911-24) occurs perhaps more than any other in these pages. He had been an unsuccessful candidate in 1901 and came to the Headmastership when little short of fifty. Though himself a Harrovian, he had spent half his life at Winchester and had absorbed the ethos with every nerve and fibre of his remarkable being. An extraordinary person to look at, with his large ungainly figure, his bristling piratical moustaches, and his peculiarities of manner and dress, as uninhibited in his enthusiasms as he was unashamed of his emotions, he comprised a unique mixture of eccentricity and idealism which created fun and life and laughter all around him. Some thought him a fraud, impossible to take seriously, but others, great scholars like Arnold Toynbee for instance, were swept along and inspired to scale their own heights by the force of his personality.

When the Warden and Fellows decided in 1922 to extend Rendall's tenure of office for another two years, they wrote to the Second Master, A.T.P. Williams, asking him not to commit himself to any other appointment without notifying them. His promotion to the Headship (1924-34) followed as a matter of course, and the high estimate of his qualities was endorsed by his subsequent appointments as Dean of Christ Church, Bishop of Durham and finally of Winchester. Though a man of great stature both physically and intellectually, he was never overbearing or condescending, but always sympathetic, courteous, and kindly. He was not very sure of himself in dealing with boys, and when Second Master, left College largely to look after itself. But his humanity and sure judgement left their mark on the school: thanks to him the ground-ash was abolished as an instrument of punishment, the arts flourished as never before, and the modernisation of the curriculum begun by Burge was completed.

Spencer Leeson (1935-46), in spite of having been himself a Winchester scholar, brought an unusual breadth of experience to the school, having served five years with the Board of Education and then been Headmaster

Opposite: Hubert Murray Burge, Headmaster 1901-1911. 'Spy' cartoon of 1903.

of Merchant Taylors. His main task was coping with the difficulties of wartime, with the very real threat of evacuation, but he turned this to good advantage by using the emergency as a way of breaking down the school's insularity. Also as Chairman of the Headmaster's Conference for an unparalleled span of six years (1939-45) he was closely involved with the implementation of the Fleming Report which sought to integrate the independent and maintained schools. His own personal ideals were based on a fusion of Platonism and Christianity, where truth, beauty, and goodness were one. It was not fashionable even then to seek to make religion the basis of education, and it could not be said that he carried the whole school with him, but his happy ebullience was backed by a strong will, and it is due to him as much as anyone that the Education Act of 1944 still requires the day's work to begin with an act of worship.

The first postwar Headmaster was Walter Oakeshott (1946-54). A fine classical scholar, he became an expert on mediaeval book-illustration and later completed a majestic work on the Winchester Bible. He was also a gentle, caring man, loved as few other Headmasters have been; but lacking some of the steeliness which that office requires, he ended his time sadly in dispute with one of his housemasters, and while still comparatively young left to take up the Rectorship of Lincoln College, Oxford. With him Desmond Lee (1954-68) and John Thorn (1968-85) have seen the greatest transformation of all. The effects of reorganisation in the country's secondary and higher education, the changes in society, the revolutions in moral and cultural values, have all had to be absorbed and the course adjusted accordingly.

It is impossible to predict what the way ahead into the next century will be, but it is reassuring to have six hundred years of experience behind one. It helps to see things in perspective. Consider how tenuous the school's existence must have seemed when Thomas Cromwell was dining in the Warden's Lodgings, when James I evicted the Fellows and scholars to house his Court, when Plague swept the city of Winchester and the boys were evacuated to Crawley, when the militia had to be called in to suppress rebellion, or when Lord Clarendon was collecting his evidence of the misuse of charitable funds by Public Schools.

Chapter II

Buildings and Development

This chapter is not intended simply to be a gazetteer of the buildings and plant, drawing your attention to the fine architectural detail of the Chapel vaulting, the glowing colours of the mediaeval glass, the bosses in the Chantry roof and so on. There are enough printed guides readily available to fulfil that need. In pursuance of the general purpose of this book, to show how changing pressures and priorities have affected the life of the school, attention is rather focused on the ways whereby the different stages of development have come about; how planning and chance, philanthropy and economic necessity have helped to shape the immediate environment.

As a starting point we shall take the year 1866, when George Moberly's long and eventful headmastership came to an end. The old College buildings were still much as they had been in mediaeval times, with scholars and Fellows (a few at any rate) occupying their respective chambers, and the rest of the main court taken up with the kitchen, Hall, and Chapel. In the outer court there had been changes. The Brewery and Stables were still in use, but the slaughterhouse in the north-west corner had long ceased to function (1697), and the granary had been absorbed by the extensions to the Warden's Lodgings fronted by a new Gothic facade in 1832-3.

Living conditions in College were primitive. The scholars slept in their ground-floor chambers, many of them on the wooden bedsteads which Dean Fleshmonger "calling to mind the evils and discomforts which he had suffered as a child" had presented in 1539-40. The lavatories were earth-closets without doors, and the only concession to modernity had been the provision of running water in 1837-9. The diet in Hall consisted largely of meat, bread, and beer, as it had always done. The regular dish was mutton, and the pet names for the different cuts conjure up horrid images of what it was like: Cat's Head, Cut, Fat Flab, Fleshy, Long Dispar, Middle Cut, Rack. On meatless holidays, a solid indigestible lump was served whose ingredients seem to combine those of Suet Dumplings and Bread and Butter Pudding.

In 1657 the scholars had been provided with a Sick House of their own, and that was an improvement on the days when the stricken had simply stayed abed in the chambers which they shared with their healthier colleagues. In times of pestilence all or part of the school might be evacuated to a country retreat, most usually to Moundsmere where the tenant of the manor was until 1887 bound by his lease to set aside rooms for this purpose.

The facilities for the fee-paying Commoners quartered outside the main buildings were little better. In 1739 the Headmaster John Burton had purchased the lease of the mediaeval Sisters Hospital just to the west of the College. Onto this he built dormitories, a sick-room, a hall, and whatever else was necessary for accommodating a hundred boys, as well as a new house for himself on the College Street frontage. Those buildings, together with the former Sisters Chapel adjacent to the College Brewery, constituted Old Commoners, a labyrinthine jungle which, in spite of being dirty, uncomfortable, ill-ventilated, ramshackle, crowded and impossible to superintend, possessed an irresistible appeal for all those who came to know it. Living there was an adventure in itself. But, ironically in view of later events, Moberly considered it unhealthy, and resolved to rebuild the whole complex. He started in 1839 by making for himself a new house on a scale that was a positive inducement to increase the number of his children, then seven or eight, to its final total of fifteen. It occupied about the same amount of space as the building he then put up to house all the Commoners. The costs for the whole project were to have been met by public subscription, but when this failed to produce more than about a third of the sum needed, the Warden and Fellows stepped in, and with uncharacteristic generosity contributed £7,000 of their own and loaned the balance of £10,000 to Moberly at 3½%. The stringent cost cutting in the Commoner building resulted in "a mean block that resembled a cheap nineteenth century workhouse" a structure than which "the heart of man never brought forth anything more irredeemably hideous". Such was the judgement of contemporaries. And it did not just look awful: it proved to be a death trap as well. The ventilation was totally inadequate and, with the streams that flowed under the building choked by rubble, there was no effective drainage. Every summer the germs happily multiplied and sickness struck, as Moberly's diary dramatically testified: "July 1843. The end of the half-year, and how much to think of. Scarlet fever, with the dispersion of the boys, and no death in the house, nor infection to my own. Poor Hooper died after he went home." After a particularly virulent outbreak in the hot summer of 1846 many parents withdrew their sons from the school in alarm, and the number of Commoners slumped from 143 to 40.

The worst evils were remedied by making quite simple alterations, but as the numbers started to rise again to their previous levels Moberly, fearful of the effects of overcrowding, turned to the idea of having separate boarding

Old Commoners 1739-1839. (Above) the Cloister Gallery and Headmaster's House built by John Burton. (Below) the mediaeval hospital converted into Common Rooms, dormitories etc. Engraving by Richard Baigent (1838) the school's Drawing Master.

houses. He intended, he said, to retain 100 Commoners under his own control and divide another 100 among four houses. In fact only three were founded during his term of office. Two made use of existing houses owned by members of the staff, Chernocke House in St. Thomas Street, and what is now called Moberly's in Kingsgate Street. The third was opened on Southgate Hill in 1862, the first to be custom-built, and that was a piece of speculation on borrowed capital by the Rev. James Du Boulay, the Headmaster not having been able to guarantee him any boarders at all.

In 1866 the total number of boys in the school, scholars and Commoners together, was 285. Their teaching was mostly done in School, a large rectangular, brick building of 1687 decorated in the style of Christopher Wren who was constructing a palace for Charles II only a few hundred yards away at the time. To cater for increased numbers and the study of mathematics, an unsightly annexe had been tacked onto the western end in 1833.

For their recreation the boys' principal play-area was Meads, which had originally been used as a farm, then as a park for the Fellows who relinquished their claim to it in 1790; it was now available to Commoners and College alike since the wall separating the two of them had been taken down in 1862 to make way for the Fives Courts donated by George Ridding's father. Commoners also had a field of their own on the other side of the canal, on land later buried beneath the railway embankment. For everyone there were also the regular processions up onto St. Catherine's Hill, as yet unspoilt by railway or by-pass road, for badger-hunts, free fights, cricket and football matches, running races, tree-climbing, collecting wild flowers (for which Moberly gave a prize, the closest he got to sponsoring the study of Natural Science), bird-snaring and fossiling.

This was the Winchester that Ridding found, and not much of it satisfied him. His immediate aims were to increase the number of Commoners and give them better accommodation, to improve and enlarge the teaching facilities, and to provide more space for playing games. Since he could expect little support from an unregenerate Governing Body, he had to put his hand deep into his own pocket. For about £3,000 he bought the 6.5 acres of Culver Close, prepared it for building, and then leased it out in four equal plots to the young men who were to start boarding houses there. They each needed about £7,000 in capital for the building operation, and then paid Ridding £400 rent. It was a business arrangement rather than an educational one, with large profits to be made out of the Commoners' fees.

In the summer of 1869 the new houses were ready; in addition Southgate House had been enlarged for C.H. Hawkins to take boarders, and Sunnyside in Compton Road was being prepared for E.J. Turner. The Commoners could now move out of their cramped and insalubrious quarters which,

Photograph of 1885 showing Domum Cottages, the canal, and the Boat House. On the left is part of the Commoner Field with the railway embankment under construction; St. Catherine's Hill is in the background.

for only £500 in building costs and twice that amount in paint, underwent speedy conversion into a set of classrooms. School was left untenanted and the annexe demolished.

To make more playing-fields Ridding had two areas of land south of Meads wall cleared, drained, and levelled. Here in 1870 the annual cricket match against Eton provided the best possible inaugural celebration by bringing to an end a dismal run of ten defeats.

All this, and more, was accomplished within the first five years of Ridding's rule. It is estimated that he spent about £15,000 of his own money on such projects, and although he was not poorly off — his annual income was around £4,000, he had no dependents since his wife had died childless, and Income Tax was around 1.5p in the pound — yet this was munificence on a heroic scale.

When the newly constituted Governing Body came into office in 1871, they were faced with something of a problem. A considerable portion of the school's property was now in private hands (though rather meanly they still insisted that Ridding pay them rent for the playing-fields he had created), and it would not serve the best educational ends to have the Headmaster and housemasters carrying such a large financial commitment. Fortunately the circumstances favoured a take-over, as disagreements were already arising about how the expenses and profits were to be shared between landlord and tenant. After two years of negotiation the College in 1874 purchased Culver Close from Ridding, and eight of the nine houses, for £53,700; the ninth housemaster, E.W. Sergeant, held out for a higher valuation before agreeing to sell five years later.

From that time onwards the Governing Body has had control of all building development, whether the initiative has come from inside or outside the school, whether financed by their own resources, by gift, or by appeal. But the mouths of gift-horses have not always received close enough inspection, and a building has a permanency that leaves ample leisure for repentance.

Many of the school's sports facilities have been provided by individuals. Ridding continued as he had begun by paying for a Rackets Court (1872), more Fives Courts (1882), misleadingly called Bear Cages as if Fearon had been their donor, and improvements to the stretch of river called Gunner's Hole where bathing took place (1874). Private generosity in later years has helped to pay for all the main pavilions — in 1930 the one built in Meads as a tribute to Jack Frazer who died in a skiing accident, and another in New Field presented by the Hunter family to replace Webbe Tent (1887); the Squash Courts (McHardy 1931, Colman 1956); and a miniature shooting range, a memorial to George Cecil who was killed on 1 September 1914, felicitously opened with a bull's eye by Rudyard Kipling in the following year. The cost of turfing Delta Field, down by the railway embankment, for football pitches was wholly borne by Eustace Palmer in 1923, and the field thereby acquired his name. But by far the largest benefaction of this century was in 1922 when the area south of St. Catherine's Hill, known as Twyford Down, and including the Hockley Golf Course, was put up for sale. An appeal to the Governing Body to try and secure it for the school had failed: the asking price was over £10,000 and they had no such funds available. A builder was already marking out the land in plots for development when two bachelor masters stepped in and bought it. They were Murray Hicks, who served the school for 37 years as teacher and housemaster, and Maurice Platnauer, later Principal of Brasenose College, Oxford. They leased the land at no profit to themselves but considerable advantage to the College which enjoyed preferential rates for use of the Golf Course. Then in 1955 they handed the whole lot, now extended to about 500 acres, over to the school, with the admirable proviso that the disposal of the rents was to be entirely at the Headmaster's discretion.

Recent gifts have also added to the beauty of certain parts of the buildings, like the magnificent aluminium and glass doors for Chapel donated in 1967 in memory of Philip Williams, and the panels of mediaeval stained glass from the original Jesse window, which were taken out for cleaning in 1821-3, then dispersed and lost, until the detective work of Herbert Chitty, the technical skill of Dennis King, and the generosity of Kenneth Clark recovered and restored them to Thurburn's Chantry in 1951; five more figures were bequeathed by Otto von Kienbusch of New York and installed in Fromond's Chantry in 1978.

But generosity on the scale of the Twyford Down benefaction is hardly to be expected in an era of very high taxation. These days larger projects that cannot be financed from the College's own resources have to rely on corporate giving in response to a general appeal. Such was the method by which School came to be built in 1683-7, and it has been used many times since. The question might well be asked why a school like Winchester with its large endowments should ever need to call upon outside help at all. The answer is that under the Universities and College Estates Act of 1925 the school is bound to repay over a period of years any capital sum that it takes from its endowments to spend on improvements. So it is in the curious position of being able to make loans to itself but then requiring more money to service that loan. In those circumstances an Appeal is preferable to a large fee-increase.

Appeals are usually of two sorts. The first is where a specific sum is sought for a specific objective, be it utilitarian or commemorative. By this means were financed the South African War Memorial Gate, whose foundation stone together with a casket containing a copy of *The Times* for the day was laid by Lord Roberts in pouring rain on 9 October 1902; the present Fives Courts and a second Rackets Court completed in 1910 although the subscription list had originally been opened twenty years before; and more recently the gates into New Field honouring Harry Altham (1971) and the pavilion in memory of Rockley Wilson (1966). In this category too perhaps should be placed the gift — or more properly the transfer at a nominal cost — of St. Catherine's Hill which the Old Wykehamist Lodge of Freemasons purchased from the Ecclesiastical Commissioners in 1930 in order to ensure that the access to which Wykehamists had assumed a right for centuries should be properly theirs in perpetuity.

Of more general importance however are the open-ended Appeals for a range of objectives. In 1893 the College celebrated the 500th anniversary of its opening: actually they were a year out owing to a misunderstanding of the mediaeval dating — it should have been 1894 — but that was not discovered until after the event. Clearly there had to be some permanent memorial of the occasion, and discussion began in good time. Potential trouble however lay in the fact that the Warden and Fellows left the recommendations to a committee of eighty-nine Old Wykehamists, and agreement proved very elusive. In 1890 a scheme for restoring Chapel was suggested; by the end of the following year this had grown to a proposal for building a whole additional Chapel projecting into the Warden's Garden. An imaginative idea floated by H.A.L. Fisher for founding a new secondary school instead "met with a distinctly cold reception"; he was after all a person who could later speak of Wykehamists as having "minds rotted with piety" and his views on Public School religion were hardly to be considered sound. So an architect for the new Chapel was engaged to draw up preliminary plans, but in November 1892 the scheme foundered on the rocks of dissension and the Warden and Fellows told the committee to think again. At a meeting in March 1893 the first proposal was for the restoration of the Founder's Chantry in the Cathedral, the refurbishing of College Hall, and the provision of the new Rackets Court which had been promised since 1889. But by this time another idea, eloquently promoted by F.G. Kenyon who was later to be Director of the British Museum, had caught the general interest: this was to build "a group of memorial buildings for the preservation of Wykehamical antiquities, and the encouragement of Art, Architecture, Natural History and other Sciences." In retrospect this bears the unhappy stamp of compromise upon it, designed to satisfy the traditionalists who wanted to embalm the past, the promoters of the Arts who were disappointed that nothing had come of the promises made years before in Ridding's time to provide room for Drawing and Music, and the progressives who wanted to see Winchester properly equipped for Science teaching.

A subscription list was opened but the expected flood of donations did not occur and less than half of the ten thousand pound target was realized in the first year. There had been too much disagreement, and now there was even more about the site to be used; should it be in place of the Headmaster's stables (where the Fives Courts are now), in the Warden's vegetable garden (where New Hall stands), adjacent to School or the classrooms? In the end they settled for the ground in front of the Gymnasium in spite of very proper objections about the crushing effect of its proximity to College Sickhouse. Fearon then got to work on the reluctant subscribers and by June 1897, when the building was officially opened, all but £500 of the final £12,500 cost had been met by the appeal.

Unfortunately the initial enthusiasm did not last very long. By 1904 the scientific need had been met much more efficiently by a new Science Building, and the Natural History Society was on the wane. Even the Art facilities proved inadequate, and were for a time actually relocated above Chantry. Within a single generation there was serious consideration of moving the whole building; but it still stands, an expensive neo-Brunelleschian monument to the dangers of unplanned development: a mistake, well-intentioned, but a mistake nonetheless.

Museum, built by public subscription and completed in 1897, in celebration of the school's 500th anniversary.
(Photograph: M. Dyckhoff)

Such a judgement is harder to make about the structure that stands beside it, the War Cloister designed by Herbert Baker and dedicated in 1924. Architecturally it is a fine addition to the complex of school buildings, and it is as noble a memorial as one could wish to the hundreds of Wykehamist dead from two World Wars. But seen in the context of a school, a place of education, it may seem to some people, as it did at the time, to exemplify the principle of "conspicuous waste". Built of the finest materials throughout, knapped flints, dressed stone, and English oak, it must be one of the most extravagant private War Memorials in the country. And it should be remembered that the cloister was never intended to be more than a part of the whole scheme; only when the full cost became apparent were the more utilitarian features dropped.

Monty Rendall, to whose supercharged emotions the War brought a conflict of unimaginable intensity between patriotic pride and personal sadness, was already thinking about suitable memorials in the summer of 1915: a scheme for educating the sons of fallen officers, and a new School Hall, he suggested. A year later his plans had taken on more definite shape. There was to be a gate, flanked by two halls and joined to Kingsgate Street by a double cloister. One hall would be a war Museum, the other a Senior Common Room (his comment that "the present Masters' Common Room is sunless and inadequate for the increased staff" deserves a passing smile; it took sixty-five more years and a further doubling of the staff before any extra room was found).

In 1917 it was time to try the idea out on the Old Wykehamists themselves, and Rendall set out in person for the Western Front with his mission. A meeting was arranged at Amiens and, with the collusion of G.H.Q., Wykehamists had no difficulty in getting passes for the evening, in spite of the imminence of the battle of Cambrai. The Old Wykehamist dinner which took place that evening on 17 November at the Salons Godbert was surely the most remarkable there has ever been. The hundred guests could not but be aware of the supreme irony that they were assembled to discuss what could well be a monument to their own deaths. "For this reason," a survivor sixty years later recalled, "the proposal that funds should be set aside for the education at Winchester of the sons of Wykehamists killed in the war received more support and attracted more interest than the proposal to build the Cloisters. Actually there was very little discussion about the War Memorial, everybody being keen to get on with the real business of having an enjoyable evening."

When the war was over and Herbert Baker's plans published, there were many who felt the scheme to be "grandiose, expensive, and unnecessary" and Lord Parmoor's voice was but the most authoritative of those who suggested that such expenditure could only be justified if some educational purpose was to be achieved. The majority of Wykehamists even so was in favour of going ahead with the project, but in spite of the large sums of money promised it was soon clear that the complete operation would be far too expensive. In order to retain an adequate sum for helping sons of Wykehamists through the school, only one building could be erected — and that, they finally decided, should be the War Memorial Cloister. Work started in 1922 and was finished in two years, Rendall's term of office having been specially extended in order to see it through. The ceremony of dedication was carried out on 31 May 1924 by the Duke of Connaught, who described it as "one of the most unique that has happened in our days"; then followed an address delivered with rather greater eloquence by the former Foreign Secretary, Lord Grey of Fallodon.

The Cloisters cost £65,000 at a time when the Winchester fees were £210 a year, and it is not improper to wonder about other uses to which such a sum might have been put. Another boarding house, a proper School

Lord Grey of Fallodon speaking at the dedication of the foundation stone of War Cloister in 1922.

Hall, more bursaries? In fact when the bills had been paid and grants made for the education of the sons of the fallen, there was still a residue of over £10,000. This was earmarked for the eventual construction of the hall which the school had been asking for since 1878. In 1928 R.M.Y. Gleadowe, the Art Master and designer, made sketches of a building to seat 1,000 people with room for storing bicycles underneath. Possible sites were discussed, but without any hopes of action until more money was collected.

The money came with the Second War. The War Memorial Fund of 1946 had, and still has, as its principal object the provision of financial assistance for the education at Winchester of sons of Old Wykehamists. But there was also a substantial amount which could be set aside for a new hall when building restrictions were lifted. In 1956 Providence gave a helping hand when Sir George Cooper made his magnificent offer to restore to the school the oak panelling which had been removed from Chapel in 1874, a supreme example of the wood-carver's art by the hand of Edward Pierce. Further grants from the Pilgrim and Dulverton Trusts, which accompanied the school's undertaking to provide a fitting home for the panelling, finally made the building possible.

In 1961 New Hall — the unimaginative name justified by Wykeham's precedent at Oxford — was opened in tremendous style with a witty and colourful Masque which showed it off to best advantage. Peter Shepheard the architect was faced with an unusual problem, aesthetic as well as practical, in reconciling the requirements of a modern hall with the limitations imposed by the panels. But by general consent the interior is a triumph, and the splendour of the setting among the trees of the Warden's Garden makes it hard to see why a majority of the Fellows originally wanted to place it on the north side of War Cloisters.

Since the last war there have been three major Appeals, in 1956, 1973 and 1982, all organised and directed by the Governing Body. But that brings us into the area of Planned Development, and before dealing with them we must go back in time to the point where the Warden and Fellows first took the initiative in deciding how the school's facilities should be improved and extended by purchasing the boarding houses. Health and hygiene were two immediate priorities as their prominence in the Minute Books of the 1870's and 1880's testifies. An outbreak of typhoid in 1874 which caused one death in the school led to plans for better drainage, and five years later the College was piped into the new town system. But the earth-closets remained until the end of the century. The report of one of the many inquiries into this aspect of school life led to the suggestion in 1880 that a Sanatorium be built. Three years later William White was appointed architect, and the remarkable result of his labours became an all too prominent feature of the school landscape. Except for connoisseurs of the High Victorian Baronial style it was an unlovely thing, and was from the start very difficult to maintain and expensive to run. Boys used to pay a fixed sum each term for the upkeep, while the nursing expenses were shared among those who made use of them — and that could prove extremely costly if you were the sole patient for a month. The wards with their thirty-two beds, the separate Fever Wing, the two operating theatres, were hardly ever used to the full and long remained a costly anachronism.

If the Sanatorium proved to be an error in scale, the attempt to effect the "internal restoration" of Chapel was hardly less of an error in taste.

Photograph of c.1885 showing the Victorian development of Meads, before Museum and War Cloister were constructed. The buildings are (left to right): Sanatorium, College Sick House, Gymnasium, Rackets Court, and two blocks of Fives Courts.

Sir Giles Gilbert Scott was originally engaged for the work in 1874, but he resigned on the grounds of professional etiquette as William Butterfield had already become a more or less permanent architectural adviser to the College. Butterfield did not originally intend to remove the decorative panelling which Warden Nicholas had installed in 1680-3 — "I am no fanatic in matters of that kind," he said — but the need to provide more seats, and curiosity about the possible existence of mediaeval painting on the covered walls led to the disastrous decision to strip the chapel bare. The panelling, which had cost about £1100 at the time of its manufacture two centuries earlier, was dumped in Meads and then sold in two lots for £30 a piece to the Rev. H. Yeatman. Since he was unable to use it as he had hoped, it sat for some years in a barn, then passed through an extraordinary series of situations, gracing a laundry, a Skating Rink, and a Drill Hall, before being fitted into Hursley Park; thence it was finally transferred by the munificence of Sir George Cooper to become the glory of New Hall.

In other respects the improvements wrought by the late Victorian Fellows were more successful. The teaching staff in 1877 were so eager to have a proper gymnasium that they were prepared to lend the money themselves, but the Governing Body preferred to make a capitation charge on the boys and pay the balance from school funds. The gym is sometimes represented as having been provided by Ridding personally, but in fact it was the first structure put up by the College authorities under the new regime. By the end of the century they had also made new classrooms (1883), re-equipped School as a Concert Hall (1885) and bought Dogger's Close and Kingsgate Park for playing fields. More still was to come in the last years before the First War. The progressive ideas of H. M. Burge provided the impetus; the growing number of fee-payers and the abundance of cheap labour and materials made it practicable. In fifteen years, unaided by Appeals, the Warden and Fellows built or purchased two new boarding houses (Kingsgate House and the resited Chernocke House), Science Buildings, Music School, Armoury, and a gallery as well as a new organ and panelling for Chapel; they extended the grounds by the acquisition of Bulls Drove and Watermeadows, they created more classrooms and wrought substantial improvements to the accommodation in College.

If the next forty years give the impression of comparative inactivity, that is not surprising in view of the draining effect of two wars, but it is a little misleading just to leave it at that. Development tends to happen in cycles, and what one generation builds the next has to maintain. So the building activity of 1820-40 was followed by a dormant period 1840-70, the developments of 1870-1910 were consolidated in the years up to 1956, and now we are in the latter stages of a further programme of expansion and improvement which will last until about the end of the decade.

Between the wars there were also major refits to be done. The boarding houses were fifty years old and having to accommodate far more boys than they had been designed for. Several of them needed as much spending on them as the original purchase price. Morshead's was so far gone that in 1937 total reconstruction seemed necessary; but the estimated cost, £30,000 and rising, was more than could be found, and the onset of the war meant that they had to patch and make do. To this day successive housemasters have treasured a postcard on which is scribbled in Spencer Leeson's hand "Morshead's to be demolished and rebuilt." During these years the Warden and Fellows were also spending money judiciously on the purchase of private houses in College Street and Kingsgate Street as they came up for sale, so that all the staff could live in the immediate vicinity of the school. That has bought great social benefit, but a large annual maintenance bill.

The next phase of development began in 1956 with the launching of a major Appeal for half a million pounds. The objectives came mainly under the heading of "modernization" but there was also to be a new playing-field, called after Warden Gater, and an extension to the Science Buildings. At the same time the long-awaited New Hall began.

The 1960s brought a Modern Language laboratory, the Physical Education Centre, and a Theatre Workshop, which are described in later chapters, and by 1970 the boarding houses had all been embellished by the addition of study accommodation for about a third of the inmates. But the 1956 Appeal had fallen some way short of its target, and with its present buildings now brought properly up to date it was time for the school to be looking towards the needs of its next generation who would be more in number, requiring better cultural and artistic facilities and a lot fewer sick-beds.

So a second Appeal was launched in October 1973, with the new boarding house and sanatorium as its main, though not most immediate, objectives. The political whirlwind of the next few months blew away most of the expectations. With oil prices and inflation rates leaping upwards as fast as the Ordinary Share index declined, all the cost-projections became quite unrealistic, and although the Appeal succeeded in raising nearly all the money it had asked for, only the first stage of operations could be carried through. By this means the school has acquired a superb library extension thanks to the personal generosity of the Makins and Blackwell families; more classrooms and laboratories, both scientific and linguistic; and an additional wing for Music School. At the same time the Chambers in College were given new oak fittings which combine comfort with dignity in a manner that has deservedly won commendation from the Worshipful Company of Carpenters for their "design, choice of timber, manufacture, installation, finish, and behaviour."

In spite of the financial difficulties, the main building projects, for a new sanatorium and boarding house, both reached quite an advanced stage of planning before being, for different reasons, laid aside. The sanatorium designs entailed much too great an expense, and the conversion of an existing building seemed to offer a more reasonable alternative. The corollary of this scheme was the redevelopment of the site of the present sanatorium. The architect Ted Cullinan produced designs which fitted two boarding houses into the vacant space. The Warden and Fellows liked the plan, and rumours that it was to be put in hand immediately even reached the front page of *The Times*. But in the end the objections of the teaching staff were decisive: while applauding the ingenuity and architectural integrity of the design, they criticized the overcrowding and lack of privacy that it entailed. That was still not the end, for committees now got to work to decide what they *would* like a boarding house for the 1990's to comprise. That meant taking a very close look at the existing houses, and before the investigation had gone far, it had become apparent that the old would need a complete overhaul before the new could even be contemplated.

*Accommodation for Collegemen and Commoners improved by the 1973
Development Appeal. (Above) Seventh Chamber in College, (below) a study
in Moberly's. (Photographs: E.A. Sollars)*

Benefactions from the Makins family. (Above) new Physics laboratory, (below) the Makins Room, an extension of the Library.

The process of reconstruction began in 1979 with Moberly's. More studies were added, recreational facilities were improved, and standards of health and safety brought up to the level demanded by local inspectors. The other houses were similarly overhauled in the course of the next eight years. As all the building renovation was carried out while the houses were still occupied, the difficulties for the housemasters, the inmates and the workforce were immense. But at the end of it the numbers in the school had increased by fifty, the boys had more privacy and greater comfort, and prospective parents could be shown the changing rooms with pride and not apology.

At the same time development was under way in other parts of the campus. The Theatre Workshop which had been created out of the old Gymnasium in 1969 (see p.140) was upgraded to become the Queen Elizabeth II Theatre. The design was by Tony Peake of the Cullinan partnership, and the name was conferred after Her Majesty had attended an inaugural performance of the Revue written for the Sixth Centenary celebrations.

The same firm of architects produced a wonderfully imaginative conversion of the unpromising Sanatorium building into an Art School which would be the envy of many specialist colleges. It was opened by the Duke of Gloucester in March 1985. The Sanatorium itself moved in 1982 to less pretentious premises in the south west corner of Kingsgate Park.

Both the old and the new fabric profited from the development. Chapel was given a new organ, and Science School a further extension to house a better library and lecture theatre, and rooms for computing and electronics.

Over eight years the whole programme cost more than eight million pounds. The Sixth Centenary appeal raised one and a half million: the rest had to come from deployment of capital money. The scale of the whole operation was, in adjusted monetary terms, greater than any undertaken in the history of the school since its foundation.

Chapter III

The Social Order

The society which Wykeham founded was to be under the care of a *Custos* or Warden, who was to have charge of the "persons, possessions, substance, and goods" of the College. In plainer terms he had an overall responsibility for the election and conduct of Fellows, masters, and scholars, the administration of the estates, the implementation of the statutes, and the maintenance of the buildings and fittings. The Warden was appointed for life, and only gross neglect of his duties, flagrant immorality or chronic infirmity rendered him liable to eviction. These charges could be easily enough evaded, it seems, for only in the troubled times of Mary and Elizabeth was the appointment terminated by anything other than preferment or, more usually, death. In over five hundred years there were but twenty-nine Wardens. The attractions of the post were evident. He had absolute security and almost total autonomy within the College, allowing him to be just about as idle or as energetic as he chose; he had board and lodgings provided for him on an increasingly grand scale (by 1629 his food allowance had come to include two whole sheep a week, 100 oysters every Friday, and an amazing fifteen gallons of beer daily); he even had Papal dispensation to hold a benefice at the same time as his Wardenship, and George Huntingford had no apparent difficulty in combining his long tenure of office (1789-1832) with the Bishoprics of Gloucester and Hereford.

The Warden had ten Fellows to assist him in his tasks. In addition to their regular clerical duties in Chapel as priests, they shared the administrative offices, those of Sub-Warden, Sacristan, and Bursar, between them. But although their function suggests a modern equivalence to a Cathedral Chapter, one should not get too exalted an idea of their character. The statutes, after all, had to ban them from keeping hunting-dogs, ferrets, or hawks, from carrying arms, letting their hair or beard grow long, or wearing tasselled hoods or pointed shoes; and on no account whatsoever were they to have red or green boots. A string of crimes which rendered them liable to expulsion included simony, heresy, theft, murder, adultery, incest, fornication, conspiracy, and assault on other members of the College.

Like the Warden, the Fellows came to wax fat on the moneys that accrued from the estates without feeling the need to put themselves under any but their statutory obligations to the children under their care. Admittedly they still had to put up with the primitive living conditions of the mediaeval chambers, while the Warden, so one of the them complained (c.1740) had built himself a nice house with "at least three parts of the site of the College appropriated to his pleasure or profit." But even if their official scale of allowances was still modest, they derived a large additional income from the fines on renewed leases, and had, since the Reformation, so little to do in return that many of them ceased to reside in College at all.

It would be an exaggeration to say that the Warden and Fellows did nothing at all to improve the quality of life for the schoolboys between 1394 and 1870, but corporate acts of benevolence are notably rare — there was the cession of Meads for their recreation (1790), grants towards the buildings of new premises for the Commoners (1739 and 1839), and the provision of extra classrooms as School was outgrown (1833), but that was about all. The school has more reason to be thankful for the generosity of individual Wardens — Robert Thurburn (1413-50) who made gifts of land to finance the building of his Chantry on the south side of Chapel, John Harris (1630-58) who provided the scholars with Bethesda, their Sickhouse, and above all John Nicholas (1679-1712) who not only had the interior of chapel fitted with the carved panelling which now adorns New Hall, but also paid from his own pocket a sum of nearly £1500 towards the cost of building School in 1687. A public appeal for subscriptions had raised only £1100, the Headmaster William Harris having contributed £100, and the ten Fellows between them a mere £130.

During the 19th century there were two Wardens who played a prominent part in the running of the school, George Huntingford who for his handling of the rebellions in 1793 and 1818 earned himself a memorable though harsh judgement in Budge Firth's history as "a lickspittle to the great and a bully to the young, a pedant, a liar and a cheat" and Robert Barter (1832-61) whose name will be recalled with greater affection in later chapters.

In theory the Warden and Fellows functioned as a Governing Body, but as few of the Fellows paid more than occasional visits to Winchester, their involvement was slight, and the management of the school was left in the hands of the Headmaster and Warden. And yet in the year 1860 the ten Fellows divided between them the sum of £6,598 in fines and allowances: the Warden's personal cut was £1,750. The Headmaster George Moberly, though he worked closely with Warden Barter and reckoned him a friend, claimed to be hardly aware of the presence of the Fellows at all

George Huntingford, Warden 1789-1832. The engraving is from a portrait by Thomas Lawrence which hangs in College Hall.

except sometimes as an irritating source of obstruction when he wanted to make new appointments.

This corrupt and unsatisfactory state of affairs could not be expected to survive the sweep of Victorian reforming zeal. The Royal Commission set up in 1861 under Lord Clarendon to investigate "the revenue and management of certain colleges and schools" made recommendations which were incorporated in a Public Schools Act (1868). This gave Governing Bodies a year to reconstitute themselves on a proper business-like footing; failing that — and it is not altogether surprising that the Fellows of Winchester failed to stir themselves an inch — the Government would intervene. Accordingly in 1871 a new set of Fellows was appointed; they included the Warden of New College, and nominees of the Lord Chief Justice, the Universities of Oxford and Cambridge, the Royal Society, and the Winchester Masters. The seven existing Fellows of the old regime were allowed to retain their status until death. The Rev. Gilbert Heathcote, who had been appointed over thirty years before, took advantage of the offer by lingering on until 1893; but the last of the resident Wardens, Godfrey Bolles Lee, who had only entered office in 1861, clung tenaciously to his life, his lodgings, and his prerogatives for ten years beyond that. By a remarkable coincidence both he and the even older Warden Sewell of New College died on the same January day in 1903, and the last representatives of ancient misrule were gone. New College thereupon gave up its statutory right to elect the Warden of Winchester, in return for having an extra representative on the Governing Body — a privilege that it still retains as a symbol of the joint-heritage.

The Fellows are now non-resident and no longer live off the College revenues. Wardens, whom they elect from among their own number, hold office for a limited period, not usually more than five years, and though they still have the use of the Lodgings when they are in Winchester, their visits tend to be limited by formal, social, or administrative obligations. Only during the last war, when Harold Baker combined the offices of Warden and Bursar, was there any more extended stay.

The Warden and Fellows do not impinge much on the day-to-day life of the school. The Warden is seen around the place often enough to be widely known, but some Fellows may only be in Winchester two or three times a year. Apart from the scholars who have their company for lunch in College Hall on the days of their meetings, and such school prefects as may have been invited to dinner with them, few boys would even recognise them. Furthermore since their dealings are almost entirely with the Headmaster, other members of the teaching staff are liable to find that their contact is only of the most distant kind. This did not matter much in the days before anyone had heard of "open government": the governors' business was mostly concerned with estates and finances, and these were not things about which the teachers needed to bother themselves. By reviving traditional notions of hospitality, Wardens of the last fifteen years have done something to bring different members of the community together. But there were still people who felt that social contact on its own was not enough. When the Warden and Fellows sold the Malory manuscript in 1976 to provide money for bursaries (see p.39), the teaching staff was not in general opposed to the scheme, but even so they made it clear that they did not like to be left unconsulted on matters affecting the future of the whole school. Since then major decisions, on the redevelopment of the boarding houses, on centralised cooking or feeding, and even on salary scales, have all been preceded by full discussion with the parties concerned. It is time consuming, but good for working relationships.

Of Headmasters I have written in the first two chapters, and their names will recur throughout the rest of this book. The other master provided for at the foundation, the *Hostiarius* or Usher, was not a person of much consequence for the first four centuries or so. Wykeham seems to have intended the post originally for young inexperienced teachers on their way to more responsible positions, the average tenure of office until 1650 being only about five years. Not until additional assistant masters appeared on the scene was he dignified by the title of Second Master, and he continued to hold a markedly subordinate rank, lodging sometimes in College, sometimes among the Commoners, until 1784 when William Stanley Goddard was appointed with a specific brief to be the scholars' resident housemaster; and that has been the Second Master's principal role ever since. He has also since then lived in the lodgings in the north-west corner of Chamber Court amid constant reminders of the debt he owes to the Headmaster John Burton (1724-66) for the embellishments that he wrought during his period of occupation.

There is no reliable evidence for the existence of any assistant masters at Winchester until 1738. However, since it was difficult for two adults on their own to supervise the work of 70 boys, let alone 150, Wykeham had determined that in each of the Chambers there should be three older scholars to keep an eye on the studies of the juniors. This system of boy-tutors, who were later paid for their services, was not formally ended until 1940, and still persists in a modified form in some Commoner houses. However it was largely superseded by the introduction of Commoner Tutors in the early 19th century, young men whom the Headmaster employed at his own expense to help him explicitly with going through the Latin compositions of the Commoners in his charge. The scholars had a similar academic tutor in College from 1836 to 1867.

The number of staff did not increase significantly until the curriculum began to widen, as described in the next chapter. When George Moberly began as Headmaster in 1836 there were seven teachers including himself for 195 boys; when he left thirty years later, there were sixteen for 285. Now (1988) there are over 80 full time teachers and 650 boys. Even so, over the whole period since 1867, there have been only about 280 people appointed to the permanent teaching staff. Many of the earlier ones were themselves Wykehamists (over a third of the first hundred, whereas the last fifty have only included two). But there was no particular social exclusiveness evident. As early as 1901 one ex-Grammar School boy (Burge) was appointed Headmaster just two years after another (Richardson) had retired from the Second Mastership. Far more limited was the University experience they could draw on; apart from the teachers of Art and Music virtually everyone appointed before John Thorn became Headmaster in 1968 came from Oxford or Cambridge. Nowadays the spread has widened to the extent that it has become positively unusual for a new teacher joining the staff to have been both to a Public School and to one of the ancient Universities himself. Another sign of changing attitudes is the fact that there have been women on the permanent staff since 1970. The present six include one Head of Department, and there are as many others working part time.

———————

There are as yet no female pupils in the school apart from daughters of members of the staff and the occasional bird of passage attending certain lessons in the Sixth Form. Nor, I think, has there been much change in the sort of boys who have come to Winchester this century other than what you would expect from the sociological shifts that have affected the whole country; the effect of higher taxation at one end and higher earnings at the other has been to create a larger central block, not easily identifiable as a homogeneous class, from whom almost all independent boarding school pupils are drawn. For a boy to come to Winchester, he needs a certain amount of intelligence, and his parents need a certain amount of money; but more important is that they should want to spend their money on something as intangible as education, rather than on holidays or material possessions. Other social considerations are these days largely irrelevant.

The original purpose of the school was to provide a good education

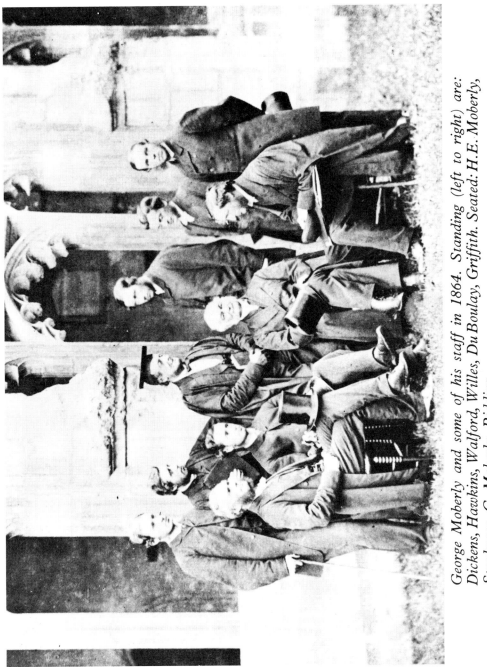

George Moberly and some of his staff in 1864. Standing (left to right) are: Dickens, Hawkins, Walford, Willes, Du Boulay, Griffith. Seated: H.E. Moberly, Stonhouse, G. Moberly, Ridding.

for nothing. Indeed there was a clear intention to exclude the wealthier classes from scholarships, and the names of the earliest pupils suggest fairly humble origins. Even in 1860 the Headmaster could claim that he had been electing to scholarships "boys of rather low parentage, with the opportunity of doing well." That was still possible at a time when the scholar's maximum fee was twenty guineas a year. In these inflationary times only two of the annual scholarships provide for a completely free education, but all the rest are still worth about two thirds of the full Commoner fee. The trouble is that the competition for these awards keeps the academic standard of the scholarship exam very high; the best preparation for it is to be found at a good private school, and that cannot but limit the field from which the scholars are drawn. Untutored genius is very hard to measure against skilfully coached competence. In recent years deliberate attempts have been made to break out of this trap. To encourage entrants from State schools, Latin is (since 1968) no longer a compulsory part of the exam, and good performances in Mathematics and Science, or English subjects, can be enough to win a place. As a result there have been boys from Comprehensive schools getting scholarships to Winchester every year since 1975.

It is a long time since anyone was actually debarred from a scholarship on the grounds of being too wealthy, and there are at the moment boys in College whose parents could afford to pay the full fees. But they are in a minority. It remains above all a place where boys of high intelligence, whatever their social backgrounds, can live among other like-minded pupils, and find the fullest encouragement to develop their particular talents.

However, the scholars make up only an eighth part of the whole school, and even in the earliest days did not constitute the entire pupil body. The sixteenth rubric of the statutes has a postscript, probably dating from not long after the foundation, which makes provision for a maximum of ten extra pupils, "the sons of noblemen and persons of influence, to be instructed in grammar without expense to the College." These were the first fee-paying Commoners. Some boarded with the Fellows, others with the scholars, a few lodged in the town from which there also came a large concourse of day-boys. By 1412 there were already about a hundred of these *extranei* ("outsiders"), a number not reached again until the 18th century.

The original requirement about social status seems to have been interpreted very widely. Hardly ever has there been any aristocratic bias in the school, except when John Burton took a dozen gentlemen Commoners into his College rooms in the 1730's, the Earls, Viscounts and Baronets whose curiously indistinguishable portraits now dominate the Second Master's Dining-Room. In the earlier part of this century many boys, to judge from their home addresses, came from a landed section of the populace that could be identified as upper middle class; in 1930 there were about thirty Wykehamists in the House of Lords, three times as many as in the

Commons. Since then financial and academic pressures have had the effect of bringing Commoners and Collegemen closer together in terms both of their social background and of their intellectual attainments. Some boys move from Commoner houses into College every year; others who might qualify for scholarships choose to accept the less valuable award of an Exhibition and remain as Commoners.

Another factor which helps to unite the two parts of the school is the bursary scheme. Such an idea was first mooted a hundred years ago — that one or two boys should be selected from local schools and maintained at Winchester out of the Exhibition fund. Fifty years on, in 1931, the Headmaster suggested that Latin might cease to be a compulsory subject in the scholarship exam, so that boys who had not been to traditional preparatory schools should not be excluded.

However nothing systematic was done until a new initiative was prompted by the 1943 Fleming Report which recommended that state-bursaries be provided to enable independent schools to recruit at least a quarter of their pupils from the maintained sector. Nothing approaching this figure was ever achieved, but two counties, Hampshire and Hertfordshire, did take up the offer of places at Winchester and for 25 years supplied a small but significant leavening. When that scheme was brought to an end by Government decree in 1975, the school determined to make up the deficiency by use of its own resources. The most precious single item in its possession, the manuscript identified by Oakeshott in 1934 as being the earliest surviving copy of Thomas Malory's *Morte d'Arthur,* was sold to the British Library to provide the money; some members of the teaching staff donated a part of their salary to the fund, and further contributions came from local industry. With the cooperation of the Hampshire Education Authority about thirty boys from local Comprehensives now apply each year for places at Winchester. A few succeed in getting on to the scholarship Election Roll, more are given assisted places in Commoner houses. In this way some six or eight boys are taken into the school every year. Since they have been through a selection process more rigorous than anyone else they tend to do very well. It needs ability, competitive instinct, and strong parental support to get them to that point. With all that in their favour, there is little problem of integration, even if they come from homes where there is no tradition of independent schooling.

It would be in accordance with the wishes of the founder and of all present members of the staff to see a Winchester education made available to any who would like it and could profit from it. But this would be impossible without sacrificing the independence that makes the place what it is. So for the time being we must be thankful that the scholarships, exhibitions, bursaries — and now the Assisted Places scheme — enable the school to take in many boys from many backgrounds who would not otherwise be able to afford it. Winchester is not, nor has ever been, simply a school for the rich. It would suffer incalculably if it were ever driven to become one.

I have so far been referring to the groups of people who make up the school community in a thoroughly impersonal way as if they were nothing more than the bricks and stone from which the place is built. But a school is a living organism whose development depends upon the way its constituent parts relate and adapt to one another. When one part is made up of adults and another of boys in different stages of adolescence, the complex of relationships, pastoral, pedagogical, disciplinary, and social, is not easily disentangled.

A manuscript book about Winchester life and language written around 1840 contains this telling remark: "The Masters have little to do with the Boys personally except to hear them their lessons". The only judgement that a boy could make about the adults who had charge of him was whether they could keep order and whether they could teach him anything. In the babel of School where at any one time perhaps 100 boys were being taught in different parts of the room, and further distractions came from the sound of the prefect's cane landing on the desk or shoulders of boys who were supposed to be engaged in their own studies, little counted except for survival. Only when proper classroom facilities were available for everyone from 1870 onwards could man and boy properly get the measure of each other.

The teachers that the discriminating pupil remembers with admiration are those of good intellectual calibre with the ability to communicate their subject and a liveliness of personality that makes instruction a pleasure. To select a few for particular mention out of so many is an invidious task, and the fact that I have chosen predominantly teachers of Classics does not indicate a personal prejudice; others will get their chance in a later chapter.

Among Headmasters the best teachers have probably been Fearon, Rendall, and Williams. Fearon was a man of prodigious industry, capable of inducing the same in his pupils, and master of all the tricks of dramatic utterance; "His voice would rise to a high tenor note, he would fling up his bearded chin, one or two warning fingers would be raised as he admonished Froude or Mahaffy for holding heretical views; as he became fired by his subject, he would tilt his chair, coil one leg round the chair leg, and slip his unemployed arm over the top of his head till he grasped the other ear". Rendall was nothing like so exact a scholar, but his personality transcended the lapses, indeed made them part of the adventure of learning. In his view, if anything was worth doing, it deserved total involvement, and little boys brought up on a severely grammatical approach to Latin poetry could not help being startled by remarks like "Ah used to sing me Horace in the early morning on the hills of northern Italy" followed by a strange mooing noise that was his idea of a suitable chant for the lyrics. His prodigious sniffs and throat-clearings and the peculiarities of his speech and appearance made him an unending source of caricature, though never of mockery; and he could communicate joy (his word) as few others. A.T.P. Williams, his successor as Headmaster, was an altogether subtler personality. Though he had the same capacity for fun, it was in him the expression of a superlatively keen mind turned upon the vain pretensions of mankind. His study of history was a probing of the human comedy; therein he found matter for amusement, without rancour or sarcasm, and translated it into the sort of epigrammatic utterance that made his hearers search their pockets for the back of an envelope on which to record it. He was incapable of a dull remark, it was said.

Fearon's successor as master of the lower Classical division in Sixth Book was E.D.A. Morshead, known as the Doidge (his second name) and no relation of Freddy Morshead who founded the fifth Commoner boarding house in 1868. He was a man with a deep knowledge and love of literature, translator of Goethe and Dante as well as Aeschylus, editor of Schiller's poems and *Childe Harold*. Fruitful digressions were at the core of his teaching method; he declared himself to be Professor of the Higher Irrelevancy. Apart from the widening of intellectual and literary awareness which he achieved in his pupils, he had a style of speech which bordered on the grotesque. Vowels underwent strange metamorphosis, and the simple word was eschewed in favour of the portentous. "Come, come," he would say to the boy who arrived late and dishevelled for early morning school with the claim that he had only just been woken up "only five minutes for cleansing, robing, and theolojay?" Someone invited to a supper of rabbit-pie and cold beef (for he and his wife, the Vulture, were a sociable pair) might be asked to "individualize the coney-tart" while he "carved the frigid ox sot". "Sot" was an appendage stuck on the end of his sentences for no discoverable purpose. He is one of the few men to have had a dictionary of his linguistic peculiarities compiled during his lifetime. The Mushri Dictionary, as it was called, went through two editions which were then consigned, quite unjustly, to the "libellous and obscene" section of the Bodleian Library at Oxford. When he left Winchester in 1903 this remarkable man retired to the slums of Southwark to spread his own particular gospel of enlightenment to the less favoured multitude.

He was replaced by Frank Carter, who gave up a professional chair at McGill University in Canada for the purpose. He was over 40 when he arrived, and in his later years, as is not uncommon with teachers, he deliberately cultivated idiosyncrasies, like the wearing of spats and the use of certain pet phrases. But he left behind generations of pupils who felt that they could never be so well taught again. Every lesson on a classical text was a performance; a textual problem evoked a masterly display of erudition laying bare the folly and ignorance of earlier editors until climactically his own solution was delivered with a finality that brooked no argument this side of the Day of Judgement. This tradition of meticulous and discriminating scholarship was maintained by John Poynton whose felicitous mastery of Latin and Greek earned him an international reputation long before his 37 years of teaching at Winchester came to an end in 1965. At the other end of the school it was a wonder to meet men with first-class minds, like Jack Parr, Malcolm Robertson (the Bobber), H. A. Jackson (the Jacker), and Hal Tyndale, devoted exclusively to the instruction of 13 and 14 year olds.

There were some light-weights and incompetents too, men who should never have been schoolmasters. War-time exigencies inevitably produced some pretty queer fish, though it is remarkable what intellectual eminence was cornered in 1914-20. Of the temporary stop-gaps four later became Fellows of the Royal Society, another Vice-Chancellor of Durham University, another was a promising mathematician called Alfred Denning, better known subsequently as Lord Denning, Master of the Rolls.

Of the later generation of dons — and it must be remembered that well over half of that 280 are still living — discretion forbids me to speak. Perhaps judgement cannot be made until our more successful pupils write their memoirs in years to come. We shall, I think, be reckoned more conscientious and industrious than our predecessors, but less colourful. The pressures are too great to allow eccentricity much scope, and it will be interesting to see how much evidence can be found to support a memorable Headmagisterial dictum that "it is a normal condition for the bachelor schoolmaster during the last fifteen years of his teaching to be in greater or less degree off his head".

Academic instruction constitutes only one part of the schoolmaster's task, for at a boarding school the teacher stands *in loco parentis* and every aspect of a boy's development is part of his care. This duty has always been recognised, but the very high ratio of pupils to teachers — for most of the school's history not less than thirty to one — inevitably meant that senior boys had to be drawn in to help. Part of the statutory obligation of the Chamber prefects was to keep an eye on the conduct of the juniors, and make sure that the master was informed of their moral development. Delation became the accepted practice, and chastisement at the hands of the authorities the consequence. However sometime towards the end of the

Frank Carter, teacher of Classics 1903-1922. Cartoon drawing by Arthur Llewellyn Smith.

18th century the right of corporal punishment, or *tunding* as it was called, was usurped by the prefects, and legitimised by the Warden shortly afterwards. As the acquisition of the weapon coincided with a sharp increase in the burden of fagging consequent upon the development of organised games which required long hours of fielding for cricket or football, the life of a small junior could become one continuous round of misery and torment. The despotism of the prefects in the first half of the 19th century was virtually unassailable.

The only remedy was increased numbers and increased care among the staff. The employment of Tutors meant that the boys had someone older to go to for help and advice, but as these young men had virtually no status they could do little to check the tyranny. Even the institution of boarding houses and the dismantling of New Commoners had no immediate effect. With one or two exceptions the housemasters kept well away from the boys' quarters: the first of them all, H.J. Wickham, signified the formality of his visits to that side of the house by always putting on a top hat for the purpose. Several of them were young, in their twenties, and new to Winchester anyway. They had put up the money for building the houses in the first place, and were effectively little more than hoteliers; indeed it was not until 1937 that they were paid a fixed salary as housemasters rather than having to depend on the profit they made from the boarding fees.

It took one outrageous incident, and a swell of public indignation in its wake to bring about much improvement in the situation. The great Tunding Row of 1872 began when an overzealous Senior Commoner Prefect, J.D. Whyte, determined to conduct a notions exam (see p.150) among the boys of E.J. Turner's house which was comparatively newly opened. The senior boy in the house, William Macpherson, refused to submit to the examination, and for this wilful disobedience was punished by having thirty cuts of a ground-ash inflicted on his back and shoulders. The father made public outcry. Ridding the Headmaster tied himself in knots trying to justify the action, a great deal of unsavoury Winchester linen was aired in the daily newspapers, and two recently appointed Fellows resigned from the Governing Body in protest at the way the affair had been handled. The beating was certainly severe (though not incapacitating), but that was not the worst feature. What disturbed people was the discovery that both Turner and Ridding had known what was happening, and had in fact been consulted by the protagonists, but had done nothing to prevent it. Ridding indeed advised Whyte against punishing Macpherson for his refusal, but left the final decision to be made by the prefectorial body. The Headmaster had not entirely abrogated his responsibility in disciplinary matters, for a boy did always have the right to appeal to him against injustice, but it was a right that was very seldom exercised. In this situation it is not surprising that an enormous number of beatings took place without any master's knowledge, about ten a week in College at one stage, and most of them for dereliction of fagging duties rather than for any moral fault.

Ridding's response to the clamour for reform was less than whole-hearted. He issued some regulations about the manner and severity of beating (a standard maximum of twelve cuts and only on the back, not the behind), but left the prefects' power virtually intact. Even so the incident was something of a watershed. Things were never so bad again, and the teaching staff started taking their pastoral responsibilities more seriously. Though Turner was too shy and Ridding too frigidly self-absorbed to win much trust from the boys, there were others about the place who could get closer to their level. Trant Bramston, one of the first housemasters, even went to the lengths of cleaning the prefects' shoes and letting them use his drawing-room as their Club. It is significant that when after a lapse of seven years the position of College Tutor was revived in 1874, his duties were no longer academic, but "to assist the Second Master in the domestic care and discipline of the Scholars." *The Wykehamist* of 1878 could talk of barriers coming down to the extent that a visitor from the past "would probably not find it easy to say which was the Master and which the Boy".

The next Headmaster, W.A. Fearon, was a more sympathetic listener than Ridding, and a generous host, as well as being the first to organise regular expeditions to London and other places of interest. At the same time, in the 1890's, "the younker" Rendall, irrepressibly boyish, was showing how infectious such enthusiasm can be, James Fort and Jack Toye were contributing on the gamesfield what C.H. Hawkins had for some years been devoting to drama and other cultural activities, and College had the benefit of a regime in which the Second Master was almost completely effaced by his wife "Mrs. Dick" who kept open house every Sunday afternoon (slabs of dough-cake and back numbers of the *Illustrated London News*), brooked no standing upon ceremony or dignity, and introduced warm draughts of humanity into the austere lives of the scholars. But they were all getting on in years. In the ten years before 1899 there were only two new appointments to the staff. The rest were mostly men in their late forties and fifties, separated by age and inclination from close involvement with the young. Boys were still ruled and on occasions tyrannized by their peers, as this letter from a sensitive seventeen year old shows: "Today I am glad to say I have had an opportunity of putting into practice my principles with regard to juniors and the ground-ash. One of Smith's most prejudiced enemies, a famous licking prefect, took the opportunity of a formal and totally inadequate excuse for telling him to come and be licked this evening with another junior. Of course everyone in College almost was savagely delighted, and the way they talked about it was sickening. Consequently I remonstrated with the man, of course to no avail. Consequently Smith

Ridding's prefects. (Left) Commoner Prefects outside the Headmaster's House (1867). (Above) College Officers (1871): Stafford Cripps' father is on the extreme left.

appealed to the Bear (Fearon) who promised to hear the case. I gave him an account of the affair, and he at once put his veto on the matter. Most of the College butchers are very bitter..."

In that incident, it will be noted, the Second Master played no part at all. However the new generation of housemasters contained more men who saw the value and importance of following where Bramston had led the way: the gentle Mottram Hewett, champion of the unathletic; James Fort, irascible but devoted; Rendall, George Blore, and others. After the First War the remarkable series of appointments made in his latter years by H.M. Burge bore fruit in the long housemasterships of the Bobber, the Jacker, Cyril Robinson, and Murray Hicks. The House became, in some cases, a castle to be defended against the assaults of the despot (in the person of the Headmaster, however benevolent), while its inmates were vigorously trained for skirmishes with the rival barons. Competition was fierce, unqualified loyalty was demanded, and the rights claimed by the housemaster over his boys were little less than proprietary. When an energetic young don persuaded some junior boys to come and play tennis with him on the town courts, their housemaster buttonholed him afterwards. "I'll thank you," he said, "to keep your hands off my pups". This autocratic style of housemastering was for the most part successful in winning the affection of the boys themselves; it is after all gratifying to know that someone is guarding your interests so jealously. It did however create tensions among the adult community, and there are stories of individuals communicating only by written messages for months at a time. Nor did it mean that all the reins of government were taken out of the boys' hands. As late as 1945 there was an occasion when a temporary don was having trouble with unruliness in his lower school div. The Prefect of Hall and Senior Commoner Prefect got to hear of it, summoned all the boys concerned, gave them a sharp lecture and threatened worse things to come. The matter was dealt with without adult intervention.

Such a thing could not have happened twenty years later. For during the 1960's a social revolution occurred, less violent at Winchester than in many other schools and universities all over Europe and the U.S.A., but significant all the same. Looking for causes, one need not go further than the analysis given by the Headmaster, Desmond Lee. At an Old Wykehamist dinner in 1963 he spoke of the new pressures on the young which made it all but impossible to maintain a conventional disciplinary rule — the relaxing of restraints at home and of moral standards in general, the insidious influence of Pop culture and teenage materialism, and the ever increasing competition for the rewards in life. Senior boys had much less interest in privilege or wish for power, especially if that just meant the imposition of regulations which they themselves regarded as petty and repressive. There was more than a suggestion that the prefectorial system would evaporate

Trant Bramston, housemaster 1869-1908, with two of his prefects, K. Wigram and H.W. Kaye, in 1893.

altogether: boys gave up their distinctive badges of rank, the ribbons and buttons and waistcoats and Morning Dress on Sundays, they took to wearing long hair and bangles and the creations of Carnaby Street, they abandoned corporal punishment and the personal fagging that had so often given rise to it, they talked of Sixth Form houses and Student Unions. In fact nothing so dramatic happened. But the burden of disciplinary responsibility was placed firmly in the hands of the masters once more, and substantial concessions had to be made in order not to upset the more important relationship of care and trust between adult and boy.

During the last fifteen years the wheel of change has moved on a few more points. The values of discipline are gently reasserting themselves, and with more general concern for the welfare of others being shown than ever before, the school is, in its seventh century, a happy place to be. John Thorn set the tone in his first sermon, advocating "an informed compassion". But he later drew attention in an article written for *The Trusty Servant* and picked up by *The Spectator*, to the dullness and lack of passion which sometimes characterizes the present schoolboy's attitudes: "Now (1978) more Wykehamists than in 1970 are thinking of how best to achieve a reasonable income level when they are 25, and fewer are moved by the Great Causes — the Third World, Conservation, Pacifism. Their aims are more familiar, and more comfortable. They are the bourgeois values of 'getting on' which over a hundred years ago John Stuart Mill feared must lead to dull conformity, to the withering of originality ... Times are easier. But providing a comfortable ride for schoolmasters is not what education should be about. Have we lost more than we have gained?"

The boy at boarding school leads an unusual life, separated for much of the time from the things that his contemporaries living at home take for granted — female company, television, parties, and so on. This is the price that he pays for membership of a community that can give him a greater concentration of opportunities for developing his intellectual, physical, and creative talents than he will ever get in his life again. But it is an artificial existence and one that imposes considerable restraints and limitations on his conduct. Some find it difficult to make the necessary adjustment, or simply refuse to do so, and there is no point in pretending that single-sex boarding education is suitable for everyone. If we leave on one side for a moment the advantages that can be claimed for such a system — they should be evident enough from what is written elsewhere in this book — and look more critically at its social effects, we can identify two questions

George Richardson, Second Master 1873-1899, and his redoubtable wife Sarah, "Mrs Dick".

that deserve separate answers. First, does the monastic life do anyone any harm? Second, would Winchester be a better school if it was desegregated?

The first invites discussion of the emotive topic of homosexuality in boarding schools, a matter which after an ages-long conspiracy of silence, has more recently received a quite disproportionate amount of attention from sociologists and journalists. That shutting a lot of adolescent boys up together for long periods does lead to some liaisons being formed is a matter not open to doubt or to surprise. But neither experience within the teaching profession nor informed psychiatric opinion leads us to believe that this is in the long term harmful or at the time any more emotionally disturbing than a heterosexual relationship between people of that age.

The second question is more interesting. Winchester was for centuries as chauvinistic as any other institution, and coeducation was unthinkable. The statutes expressly forbade any woman to set foot inside the College except a washerwoman, if a washerman could not be found, and only then if she was hideous enough to excite no suspicion. Even in the last hundred years it has been difficult for women to be accepted. Mrs. Dick could do as she pleased within her own house, but was roundly told to mind her own business when she volunteered to take charge of the College kitchen. Most surprisingly in view of his diffidence, it was her husband George who, in his retirement speech in 1899, made the first public plea for coeducation at Winchester, prophesying that in fifty years' time this would be the norm "even in the great Public Schools". He was moving faster than the times however. The idea of women's suffrage continued to be rejected as often as it was discussed by the Debating Society, and support would have been found for these trenchant words in the *New Liberal Review* of 1901: "All housemasters should be bachelors. The indispensable feminine element in each house would be supplied by the professional matron probably far better than by the random wife, and without many of her impediments to usefulness and singleness of purpose, among others being the difficulty of shelving or ousting her if found incompetent." When Monty Wright the Second Master married in 1935, it required the consent of the Governing Body for his wife Joan to take lunch in Hall with the boys.

Only in the years since the Second War has there been any joint activity with neighbouring girls' schools: a debate with St. Swithun's in 1947, then dancing classes, a madrigal society, drama, cookery, and so on. In 1970 Jennifer Gregory joined the teaching staff, the first woman to be appointed. Only recently then has it been possible to think realistically of admitting girls to the school. The cry for coeducation was loudly raised in 1965, following word of New College's intention to take in female students, and has been heard intermittently ever since. Today a straw-poll would probably find a large majority of boys and teachers favouring the change in principle. It will not happen in the immediate future, with the entry-lists full and St. Swithun's flourishing. Nor, I think, will Winchester go the way of many boys' schools and simply draft in a number of Sixth Form girls — a move that is dubious on both social and educational grounds. To do anything on a large enough scale to be worthwhile would require massive capital investment which is not possible so soon after the development programme of the 1980s. All the same a successor to George Richardson might reckon that there was a good chance of his prophecy being fulfilled before the century was out.

Chapter IV

The Pursuit of Learning

Election to a Winchester scholarship could once guarantee a subsequent scholarship to New College, a benefice, and security for life; accordingly Wykeham made thorough and careful provision for the manner in which the boys were to be chosen for his school: even the number of horses to be used by the examiners coming from Oxford was considered. However the most important point, the nature of the examination itself, was left regrettably vague. Whereas scholars for New College were to be elected in order of merit, the places at Winchester were simply to be assigned to any who seemed on examination to be "fit and suitable". From the earliest days of the school's history this laid the system open to the abuse of nomination and patronage. The outward forms continued to be observed with great punctilio until 1857 when the Oxford University Commissioners abolished the privileges of Founder's Kin, and imposed the requirement of competitive entry. But for 450 years before then the examiners, three from New College and three from Winchester, had been able to bring forward their own nominees and put them through the merest charade of an examination. This was a jealously guarded privilege: some prerogative had been exercised by Kings and by Bishops of Winchester in earlier times, but in 1726 the two Wardens, with elaborate shows of duty and courtesy, shut the door in the face of George I, and the Bishop withdrew his pretensions shortly after.

The manner of election under the old dispensation is described for us in a number of places. Here is a typical account: "I became virtually a scholar of Winchester at three days old. My father, playing whist in New College Common Room, was congratulated on the birth of his son. 'Yes' he said jestingly, 'and how pleasant if one of you some ten or twelve years hence were to nominate him on the foundation at Winchester.' A Mr. Gifford who was present took him at his word, the promise was kept in mind and carried out, and in July 1842 I went down with my father as a candidate or 'Candlestick' to the Winchester election . . . From School the Candlesticks were ushered into the Election Chamber, where sat in awful state the two Wardens, of New College and Winchester, the sub-warden, the two posers, arrayed the one in a velvet-sleeved proctor's gown, the other in a silk law-gown, and Dr. Moberly. I had prepared with great care 100 lines of Virgil, but had not construed three before the examiner said 'That will do; can you sing?' I stared, and answered 'Yes'. 'Say' he continued, 'All people that on earth do dwell'. I recited the line. 'Thank you, you may sit down.' My examination was over, and I was elected."

Two things in particular deserve notice. The first is that although the places on the Election Roll had already been bespoken, there was always a crowd of other candidates, hoping perhaps for a late extra vacancy; the other is that lip-service was still being paid to Wykeham's requirement of proficiency in plainsong. Indeed when Fearon, who had himself been a nominee scholar, became Headmaster, he reintroduced the formulaic question and answer even though by that time the competition for scholarship places was in deadly earnest.

For generations Eton had had the same nomination system, but Provost Hodgson had introduced a competitive examination in the 1840s as part of the reforms needed to attract more boys into College. The Bishop of Winchester liked the idea and suggested it to Moberly, but he preferred to stay with the old scheme until change was forced upon him by the University Commissioners. He did however have the grace to admit later that he had been wrong; and indeed the advantages were obvious. There was an end to anomalies such as happened in 1846, when a boy was elected to the Roll at the age of eight and had to leave five years later when he was still in Junior Part. In 1862 by contract there were 137 boys competing for seven vacancies, and Moberly could say with belated satisfaction "We do not know what it is to have a thoroughly stupid boy as a scholar; the school is much more widely known, and with this our connection is materially increased."

The competition for scholarships, at other schools besides Winchester, created a demand for efficient coaching, and enormous numbers of preparatory schools sprang up in the last quarter of the century. The efficiency of the best of these pushed the standard up still further, and with Winchester able, through its endowments, to finance more scholarships and of greater value than any other school besides Eton, the Winchester scholarship exam soon came to be regarded as the toughest of its kind; boys would turn down top awards elsewhere in favour of a place on the Winchester Election Roll.

The papers were from the first heavily weighted towards Classics. A child of 12 or 13 would be expected to be able to translate passages from Greek and Latin authors, to be familiar with all the niceties of grammatical form in both languages, and to compose Ciceronian prose and Ovidian verse

Winchester Scholar, from R. Ackermann's History of Winchester College (1816).

of his own with faultless accuracy and stylistic polish. There were also papers in Arithmetic (with questions of the kind "Work out .0614583 of £3 6s 8d"), Algebra and Geometry, French, and Divinity ("What do you know about Melchizedek, Gehazi, Beth-horon, Mount Ebal?" or "Quote any passages in Scripture, not from the book of Numbers, in which the name of Balaam occurs"). A combined History and Geography paper, with a distinct imperial flavour ("Write a letter from a young Englishman lately arrived in India, relating the things that struck his attention there") was included from about 1890; and English followed some twenty years later (1911). Science was not added to the schedule of papers until 1966.

Recent modifications have been designed to make the examination suitable for candidates without orthodox prep school training: the Classics papers are optional, Divinity has disappeared, and an Intelligence Test has been introduced. But the candidates, assembled yearly at Winchester as of old, are still subjected to three days of intensive written tests, and then *viva voce* interviews with their examiners. It is a process that imposes considerable strain on everyone involved, boys, parents, and teachers. The standard is a function of the demand, but the unquiet conscience is still entitled to ask whether merit can be assessed by these means alone.

For Commoners selection was entirely in the hands of the Headmaster until the first boarding houses were opened. An entrance examination was insisted upon in the Statutes published by the newly constituted Governing Body (1873), but even this was to be a hurdle, not an open competition. The same system still operates today. Candidates for Commoner entrance apply direct to a housemaster who may promise the boy a place in his house, subject to his passing the exam. Winchester is now alone among Public Schools in not making use of Common Entrance, but setting its own papers. Whether the advantage in terms of fine discrimination to be gained by such exclusiveness outweighs the off-putting effect that it has on some potential candidates, is a matter that becomes increasingly difficult to assess.

———————

The Winchester education for which pupils are prepared to compete so strenuously is partly a matter of the setting, the atmosphere, the traditions, the opportunities for physical, artistic, cultural, social. and spiritual development, which will be dealt with in subsequent chapters. But the thing that is particularly associated with Winchester is its pursuit of high academic standards, and that is what must now engage our attention.

"I suppose you are still very much a Classical school" says the inquiring

New Commoners (1839-1869) built by George Moberly and now converted into class rooms. The building on the right, an extension to School, was named Walfords after the first mathematics master. Print by Richard Baigent (1844).

visitor. By no means. It is true that John Thorn was the first Headmaster not to have a degree in Classics. It is also true that the Latin and Greek languages predominated in the curriculum for most of the nineteenth century; Mathematics was the only other subject to be taken seriously at all, and the study of Science and Modern Languages was little more than an extended joke. The timetables that were produced for the Clarendon Commissioners in 1862 showed that the boys in the Senior Division of the school had each week seven hours of Classics, with seven more for preparation, seven of Mathematics, three of Divinity (the Greek Testament, that is) and two for French and German. At the bottom of the school, the allocation was: Classics 15 (with 6 more in-school preparation hours), Divinity 2½, Mathematics 3, French 2, History 2, English 1. All nine hours of evening preparation in the bottom division were also for Classics.

The Army class, instituted by Fearon soon after his arrival, offered some slight relief for those who wanted to satisfy the high demands made by Woolwich and Sandhurst for proficiency in Mathematics and Modern Languages without having to go to a special crammer. In 1887 Fearon announced his intention of dropping Greek in the bottom division, and allowing boys into the school without it. But it was not until Burge took over in 1901 that the tyranny of the Classics was effectively diminished. He introduced for all boys in Senior Part (roughly equivalent to a modern Lower Sixth) a "staple" which included Latin and Maths, and a little bit of Science, History, and Divinity; the other nine periods a week offered a choice of more Classics, or Modern Languages, or Maths and Science. This was the beginning of the "ladder" system which still operates — A for Classics, B for Modern Subjects, and C for Science. There had been a "Parallel Division" at the top of the school since 1909 for those who wanted to do more German than Greek, and a separate division for scientists since 1921. But the ladders were the creation of Alwyn Williams, himself a History teacher of great note, soon after he had become Headmaster; they became fully established in 1930.

In the last fifty-five years, and particularly in the last fifteen, the options have multiplied enormously. A boy at the bottom of the school may now study as many as ten different subjects in a week — or thirteen if one includes Music, Art, and Physical Education. When he reaches Sixth Form level he can choose from sixteen different academic courses (and another half dozen optional extras ranging from Computer Studies to Pottery). Theoretically the number of different combinations available is over a hundred, though only about half of them make educational sense. In 1935 the ladders were peopled as follows: A 106, B 98, C 67. In 1980 the comparable figures were 38, 195, 176. But nowadays so many subjects are common to all three that the divisions are by no means exact.

So Winchester is no longer predominantly a Classical school. Rendall was the last Headmaster to believe that it could be or should be; like most of his other ideas it was a belief that amounted to a passion, and the force of his own personality was one of the things that kept the number of boys opting for Greek so high. But the growth of the new B and C ladders could only be at the expense of more traditional disciplines, and in 1938 for the first time the A ladder had fewer boys on it than either of the other two. There was another significant decline in 1962-3 when the call for technologists caused a sudden rush of recruits to the C ladder.

While Classics was still attracting a large number of specialists, Latin was the most important subject in the lower school: proficiency in Latin was what mattered most both for winning promotion up the school and for getting into it in the first place. This was not just a foolish anachronism, but based upon sound logic. For the nature of Latin, the combination of accuracy, deduction, and insight needed to master it, makes it a very good predictive subject — that is, the better you are at Latin, the better you are likely to do in other subjects. So while Latin was being taught to the limit of every boy's ability, both at his prep school and in the lower divisions at Winchester, it provided sound intellectual training and an effective measure of his capacity for more specialised work. However partly because it is a very demanding subject, partly because there is little of intrinsic interest in its early stages and it is too often taught without life or enthusiasm, it is not a very attractive one to little boys; and once the prep schools had started to diversify their efforts, introducing Science for the first time and more English subjects, once Latin had been officially demoted by being no longer compulsory for entrance either to the Universities or to the Public Schools, it rapidly lost its primacy. There are those, and not just redundant Latin teachers either, who regret its demise. No other subject has been found which can instil the same mental disciplines of linguistic precision with the same rigour and economy. But, short of a second Renaissance, nothing is going to restore its position. Winchester, with its belief in nurturing the intellect, still makes Latin a compulsory subject in the lower school, and boys who come from orthodox prep schools are expected to offer it for Entrance. Those who come, perhaps from maintained schools, without any Latin are usually given an intensive beginners' course in it, and are sometimes able to catch up in two years what others have done in five.

Greek is a more difficult language. It is absurd that it should ever have been compulsory, and nowadays it only attracts a small minority. Numbers in the lower school fluctuate between about twenty and forty at any one time, and proportionately fewer go on to study it at a more advanced level. Classics specialists are now a comparatively rare breed, even though the course is not so drily academic as it once was. Minute scrutiny of linguistic peculiarities and the cultivation of fluency in composition now take second place to a wider appreciation of the civilisations of Greece and Rome. Even if this may deprive today's classicist of the solace of Bishop Charles Wordsworth, who beguiled his declining days by turning all the Collects of the Prayer Book into Latin Elegiacs, it may also save him from the fate of Richard Carstone, the young Wykehamist character in *Bleak House*, whose schooldays fitted him for nothing in life except the production of Latin verses.

In terms of seniority and esteem Mathematics is historically the second most important academic subject. Some tuition in elementary arithmetic was given from the end of the eighteenth century onwards by the school's Writing Master, Thomas Bower. When he died in 1844, he had placed on his tombstone in Brompton churchyard the words "Late Mathematical Master of Winchester College", a title which sounded much grander than his menial status actually merited. However quite an advance was made in the 1830s. Perhaps it was due to the arrival of a vigorous new Warden, Robert Barter, in 1832. For that same year the first school prize for Mathematics was instituted by William Heathcote (candidates were expected to be self-taught in the prescribed syllabus); and in 1834 a revolutionary step was taken with the appointment of the first mathematical teacher to the staff, John Desborough Walford. Reactionaries may have been comforted by the fact that he turned down a Classical Fellowship at Cambridge in order to take up the job, and to the end of his days he avowed that Mathematics was not his favourite subject. But for forty years he devoted himself to its cause, and for two thirds of that time he carried the burden alone. Strictness combined with a compassionate nature made him an excellent teacher, and he was materially assisted in his task by having the Headmaster's full support (the same could not be said of other non-classical teachers). What guaranteed the attention of his mercenary-minded pupils was the fact that the marks even for routine maths lessons counted towards the final orders, and that there were substantial end-of-year prizes. Mathematics was also afforded some independence of status by the fact that Walford was allowed to occupy the main classroom in the extension that was already being built onto School when he arrived. It was a singular compliment that this building, unprepossessing as it may have been, should bear the name of Walford's. It was demolished in 1870 when the new classrooms were created out of the Commoner buildings. But the name John Des still lingers on as the "notion" for a certain kind of loose-leaf paper such as mathematicians might use for their rough working.

By 1870 Mathematics was well established and Walford had been joined by the vigorous if eccentric C.H. Hawkins. When Walford retired in 1873 he was replaced by "Dick" Richardson, a 3rd Wrangler and, unusually for the times, a Grammar School graduate. It has to be said that neither Hawkins nor Richardson was a particularly good teacher. Hawkins' great contributions to school life were made outside the classroom (see Chapter VII), and all

John Desborough Walford, Mathematics master 1834-1873.

that is remembered of his lessons are the excruciating puns which were his constant delight. Richardson hardly bothered with any but the abler mathematicians, and in the minds of most of his pupils his name only conjures up memories of "Dick Mons" when two hundred boys would assemble in School at the beginning of term and above the hubbub ("mons") he would roar out the names of who was in which maths sets. Somehow he never thought of posting the list and saving himself the indignity of this performance.

A new lift for Mathematics was provided by Burge's revision of the timetable, and above all by the arrival of C.V. Durell who by his work and writings dominated the teaching of Mathematics up and down the country for the first half of the century. Durell was rather an austere person, not easily befriended; his brief excursion into housemastering was not a success. But he had a brilliant mind and a genius for exposition, best displayed in his thirty or more textbooks which have been used in their millions all over the world.

The strength of its Mathematics department led Winchester to be chosen for what was to become the most successful and universally used curriculum development in the world in any subject — the S.M.P. (School Mathematics Project). Its instigator Bryan Thwaites had been a pupil and a don at Winchester before being appointed Professor of Theoretical Mechanics at Southampton. In his view "if it had not been for the willingness and enthusiasm of the then Headmaster, who was prepared to exploit to the utmost the independence of the school, the Project would have been stillborn. Never before or since has the independent sector given so much of a quantifiable kind to the nation's whole system of education."

Given that impetus, it is not surprising that Mathematics remains the school's strongest subject: that is to say, more boys study it and more masters teach it at an advanced level than any other subject.

Modern Languages have been taught at Winchester, after a fashion, for about 170 years. The earliest recorded French teacher was C.J. Belin, himself a former scholar, who learned his French as Chaplain to the British army of occupation settled in France from 1816 to 1819. He took up his appointment at Winchester the following year, though nothing is known of what he achieved. For the next fifty years the teaching of French, and from 1845 German, was entirely in the hands of foreigners. The chauvinism of the young, coupled with the fact that marks for Modern Languages counted for virtually nothing in the year's reckoning, made these lessons a farce. Schoolboys of the time gleefully recalled in later years the sport they had made of these unfortunate men — the volatile Signor Arnati, self-styled "Professor of Languages" who could always be trusted to explode at the mention of Waterloo, the amiably incompetent Herren Behr and Heller, Monsieur du Domaine, who was widely reputed to be a Southampton

A party of dons meeting in Hawkins' garden before a walking tour in Wales c.1870. Standing (left to right) are: Kensington, Were, F. Morshead, Turner, Toye. Seated: Hawkins, Richardson, Bramston.

hairdresser, and the gentle Monsieur Angoville, whose bad luck it was to have the inadequacy of his teaching and of his own English subjected to the scrutiny of the Clarendon Commissioners. "Do the boys talk French to you? — Yes — Do they talk it pretty well? — I cannot say 'pretty well' — Have you any boys in the school who speak reasonably well, with a good accent? — Yes, three or four. There are more in the school who talk, but their talking is not so good as that of those." When Fearon was asked whether he knew any French when he went to Winchester as a boy, he replied: "Yes, I do not think I knew so much when I went away."

Ridding tried to improve at least the disciplinary situation by appointing two Englishmen to teach languages, E.J. Turner and R.G.K. Wrench; both had the distinction, rare for Winchester dons, of having got 4th class degrees. These were both men who could command respect, though it would be charitable to say that the linguistic proficiency of their pupils was significantly advanced. The Headmaster's attitude to the subject could not give them much confidence either. When J.S. Furley, a fine Classical scholar, joined the staff in 1878, he was told by Ridding that he would have to take a French set. "'But I know no French, Dr. Ridding' I said. 'That does not signify,' he answered, 'it is only a matter of common sense.'"

By the end of the century there had been little progress, except that boys in the Army Class under H.C. Steel could now learn the French they needed for Cadetships. Educationally, French and German were much deader languages than the Classics. Intelligent boys could still repeat Fearon's sentiments with feeling: French teaching stopped in the top half of the school and German was substituted, but, says one, "though I was taught German during my last four years at Winchester, at the end of it I was wholly ignorant, and could neither read nor write it". Of the German Prize examination in 1897, one of the leading contestants wrote in a letter home: "The feature of the exam was that the two people neither of whom knew

Pulpiteers, the arrangement whereby the Headmaster (here George Moberly, seated left) took the top classes together in School.
Photograph of 1861.

Two classes in progress in the language laboratory (1974).

(Photograph: E.A. Sollars)

the German alphabet did the best Faust papers that have ever been done . . . Of course it was the German Unseen that pulled down my place".

Rendall introduced German into the lower part of the school as an alternative to Greek — a courageous act by someone who set so high a store by Classical education; but he regarded specialization in Modern Languages as undesirable — it was too soft an option. With one of his inspired flights of imagination he announced in the summer of 1917 that he would like to start a course in the language and culture of Russia. It came to nothing, and Russian was not taught until 1937 when Donald McLachlan, then a lively young don with radical views, fell in with the promptings of a number of Collegemen whose reaction to the growing threat of Fascism was a wish to educate themselves properly in Communist ideology.

By that time Modern Languages had at last achieved respectability after over a hundred years in the shadows. Through Rendall's time "Polly" Steel lingered on as titular Head of French. When he finally retired aged 70 in 1922, he had long outlived his usefulness. A new Headmaster, Alwyn

Williams, was determined to establish a Modern side that had parity of esteem with the traditional Classics. In 1926 he appointed a man with first class intellectual and pedagogical qualifications to be head of a properly constituted department; in fact he was the first man ever on the staff with a degree in Modern Languages.

Robin Ridgway was a brilliant teacher who achieved all that Williams had hoped. The languages lived, and yet the standards of intellectual rigour exacted were enough to satisfy the academic purists. When the full B ladder scheme came into operation in 1930, Languages and History at once became accepted as a combined discipline no less challenging, and to many more interesting, than Latin and Greek. Spanish was introduced and later Russian. A Frenchman, Jean Liétard, was brought onto the staff to add idiomatic polish. For the first time University scholarships in Modern Languages were won. The war years took Ridgway off to distinguished service in India, and McLachlan left to become Editor of the *Times Educational Supplement*. The Russian classes had to be suspended, but otherwise the fine work went on.

Since the War the department has had but four Heads, Ian McIntosh who got Russian started again and introduced Italian; Leslie Russon, joint author with his wife Agatha of several text-books, John Surry, and now Alan Conn. There is at present a permanent staff of twelve linguists, with another four working part time, and two foreign assistants. Six languages are regularly on offer (Japanese is the latest addition) and numerous others can be studied from tapes in the Language Laboratories which were first installed in 1964 and greatly improved when the old Headmaster's House was remodelled in 1974. The profusion of tongues in the school makes those days seem very distant indeed when language teachers were divided into two categories, those who knew French but could not keep order, and those who kept order but knew no French.

Of the other B ladder subjects History has been part of the school curriculum for longest. Moberly used to enjoy taking time off from the Classics to give the occasional lecture on current affairs, but when pressed by the University Commissioners to organise History teaching on a more regular basis, he showed what he thought of such interference by conducting his lessons in School before breakfast; the whole of the Sixth Form was assembled, an arrangement known as Pulpiteers, and the senior boy read to the rest extracts from Coxe's *House of Austria*. Ridding had a proper syllabus drawn up for the school, and there was the spur of annual History prizes; but it was only taught by amateurs, that is interested classicists, until the arrival in 1902 of R.D. Beloe with a degree in History and the title of History Master. Beloe's principal work however lay in starting the tenth Commoner boarding house, and in his subsequent headmastership of Bradfield. The man who gave respectability to the idea that one might be an academic historian and nothing else was Alwyn Williams, first as teacher (from which he earned himself the name History Bill), and then as Headmaster. In the generation that followed, the interest generated by teachers such as Budge Firth, Harold Walker and Tom Howarth was such that in the post-war years the number of specialists became a positive embarrassment, and the distinction of the pupils who have since become professional historians themselves is a testimony to their skills.

Geography has only had its own department and been taught as a serious academic subject since 1976. But for over a hundred years before that it had a place in the scheme of things, either as a branch of natural science, or as part of the general diet of the lower school. Physical Geography first appeared on the timetable in 1888, and was organized into a two-year cycle between the wars. There was one break in 1927 when scarlet fever struck the teaching force, and the Headmaster thought it in no way improper to invite as a replacement the President of the Royal Geographical Society. "I expect" he said, "you would find it quite amusing". And he did.

English likewise was a subject that was widely taught without being taken very seriously. Only in the last twenty years has there been a properly constituted department, or anyone on the staff who had done both parts of an English degree. Economics is the newest of the modern subjects. It was first taught at Winchester as an adjunct to Mathematics around 1930, but had to survive the disapproval of University faculties who did not like schools tampering with what they regarded as their subject. Once the credentials had been established, rapid expansion followed through the 1970's and 1980's.

The first mention of any Science teaching at Winchester is as early as 1821 when a Mr. Addams was engaged to give lectures on half-holidays. "We had one on Chemistry yesterday, and shall have one on Galvanism tomorrow," wrote a little boy to his Mama; "Mr. Addams was very entertaining; he performed several experiments and at the close of the lecture electrified us all." The initiative was not sustained. George Moberly was scornful of the educational value of Natural Science: it was only concerned with facts, he said, and "there is no germinating, fruit-bearing principle in those facts"; one might remember them today and forget them tomorrow and be no better off as a result. Even the possibility of practical applications did not impress him: "when a country gentleman begins to farm on principles of agricultural chemistry, he had better not go upon what he learnt at school from scientific lectures." The Oxford Commissioners had in 1856 suggested that Winchester should elect three scientific Fellows. The Warden blenched at the idea of an additional outlay of £1500 a year, but Moberly managed to persuade the Commissioners that it would be quite impossible to attract scientists of any consequence to a fellowship in out-of-the-way Winchester: "no one but a very small person would accept it in the first place, and such a person would grow smaller and smaller every year." By way of compromise, the school undertook to provide courses of scientific lectures by "the best lecturers of the day". What this in fact amounted to was an annual series of twelve (later ten) lectures given on Saturday afternoons in the summer term by visiting speakers. Attendance was supposed to be compulsory, but absenteeism was on a large scale. On the other hand the cost to the College was only £100 a year. The Clarendon Commissioners of 1862 showed grave disapproval of this charade, and Moberly was compelled to temper his hostility. He took a Science graduate, George Griffith, onto the staff, and detailed one of his best Classics tutors, also called Griffith (Charles), to equip himself to teach Geology - which he did to such good effect as to eclipse his other work.

Ridding was a bit more encouraging to the scientists. He helped to institute a Natural History Society, he provided a Science lecture room, bought some new apparatus, and donated a Botanical garden. He also brought onto the staff a man of real intellectual distinction in W.B.Croft, known to generations of schoolboys as The Bleader because of his second name. Croft was originally appointed as a mathematician, but after two terms Ridding sent him back to Oxford to get a degree in Science. Within a year he had a First in Physics to add to his First in Maths. The compactness of the world's scientific community at the time enabled him to keep abreast with the newest topics, such as X-rays and wireless transmission. But he was not much respected as a teacher: one of his later pupils who was himself to devote most of his life to teaching said that "he carried frigidity in the class room to a lower point on the thermometer than any schoolmaster I have ever known." Ridding could point with some pride to the winning of University Science scholarships, and to the larger number of boys in the school who now did some Science. On the other hand he argued against the Public School Commissioners who recommended that Science should be included in the examinations for entrance to Winchester, and admitted that the facilities were a long way behind those of other major schools. Chemistry could not be taught at all beyond the barest recital of facts until in 1883 new laboratories were approved, and a further addition to the staff was made. Llewellyn Larder Garbutt was undoubtedly a better schoolmaster than Croft, but he had the ill-fortune to coincide with the arrival of a traditionalist Headmaster in Fearon, and Science had to take another pace backwards for a time.

When Burge succeeded Fearon in 1901 he urged the need for a wholly new and independent Science building: it was completed in 1904 at a cost of nearly £11,000 — and well away from the other classrooms. He also coordinated a full Science teaching syllabus, and by introducing Biology as an academic subject completed the foundations of the system that still operates today.

A chemistry class with F.W. Goddard (1949)

(Photograph: A.W. Kerr)

From that time onwards the history of Science teaching at Winchester has been one of continuous development and expansion, slowly wearing away the residual prejudices among the Arts fraternity. When the first proper Science division was constituted in 1921, it was regarded as somewhat below the salt, and a newly appointed College Officer who was a scientist had to accept a nominal transfer to the Classics ladder in order to give him the dignity befitting his station. But the work of a triumvirate of Science dons, Freddy Goddard, Geoff Crompton, and Spencer Humby, who aggregated 104 years of teaching at Winchester between 1917 and 1957, ensured that the name Stinks became a term of affection rather than denigration and then disappeared altogether.

The buildings were substantially enlarged in 1927, after seven uncomfortable years when the overspill had been housed in a YMCA Nissen hut on an adjoining playing field. Again in 1955 when the Industrial Fund was offering grants for the Advancement of Scientific Education in Schools, Winchester presented one of the best cases of all the 228 schools which applied, and received one of the largest grants. This helped to pay for a new Biology block, which had further additions made to it after the 1973 Appeal, when the generosity of the Warden's son, Christopher Makins, gave us new laboratories for Physics and Chemistry as well. The subsequent microchip revolution required more space for electronics and computing, and this was provided by another three quarter million pound development in 1987-8.

During the 1960's two more teachers, Bunny Dowdeswell and John Spice, put Winchester at the centre of the Nuffield Science Teaching Project by undertaking to coordinate new courses in Biology and Physical Science. Within the school itself not only was the number of Science specialists being increased, but the subject was coming finally to be accepted as an essential part of everyone's education. As late as 1960 there had been no Science in the lower school, and only a parsimonious ration of non-specialist hours for boys on the Arts side, doubly unsatisfactory because the pupils seldom took them at all seriously, and the overworked staff could not expect to achieve much with them anyway. Now a quarter of the timetable is devoted to Science subjects for at least half his time in the school, whatever a boy's interests and future aspirations may be.

The academic reputation of Winchester rests upon its proficiency in teaching the major subjects described on the past few pages. To achieve high standards an element of specialisation is inevitable, and it is further encouraged by an educational system which requires for University entrance, concentration on only two or three subjects. These narrow requirements have for long been mitigated at Winchester by what is called the div system; this ensures that a boy shall spend at least one hour a day in his division or form, doing subjects of a general cultural or educational nature which reflect more the particular interests of his teacher than the needs of his academic programme. So the scientist may become acquainted with Plato's *Republic*, the linguist with the works of Darwin and so on. The div is the traditional pivot of a boy's curriculum, and its importance has survived even the recent concentration on teaching for exams.

A levels were until the early 1960's regarded as being of no more importance than the School Certificate a generation earlier. One could get into Oxford or Cambridge without them, and at its peak about 75% of boys in the school would do so. If a boy, and his housemaster, were persistent enough, he could win a place without having got more than half way up the school in five years. But as the academic qualifying standards at the ancient Universities rose in response to widening competition, so the need

A science lecture in the old buildings (1952).

to teach more specifically for this end increased. For good or ill A level results now provide an important yardstick in judging a school's performance, and University places are very closely linked with them. This has not been too damaging educationally as Winchester, faced with the necessity of taking these exams seriously, has been in a position to influence their content. In the past twenty years there have been in several of the major subjects modifications of the A level syllabus which Winchester dons have helped to shape, and few Heads of Department would now feel that they are being compelled to teach material which they would not themselves choose to.

In terms of statistical results the desired effect has been achieved. Twenty years ago, when there was little specific teaching for A level and the abler boys might not bother to take it at all, a pass rate of 75-80% seemed reasonable; in 1988 it was 99%. A grading system was introduced in 1963, the passes being categorized in five bands A — E. This provided a further incentive to good performance, and within a few years the percentage of A grades achieved had risen to 25%; in 1988 it was 48% representing 210 out of 433 subject-entries. However during the same period of twenty years the number of boys winning places at Oxford or Cambridge has dropped from around 70%, which was generally reckoned to be disproportionately high, to the present figure around half that. Simultaneously the number going to other Universities has increased, overtaking the Oxford and Cambridge total for the first time in 1978-9, and maintaining the percentage of leavers who go on to higher education at about 90%.

These dry figures suggest certain conclusions — that getting into Oxford and Cambridge is a great deal harder than it was, and that the efficiency of teaching in the school has if anything improved. Whether the level of intelligence among the pupils themselves has changed it is not easy to say: convincing evidence is not readily come by. College has always tended to set the pace, as one would expect; but even there standards vary from generation to generation. In terms of intellectual achievement the most illustrious decades have been the 1890's with strings of University Prizewinners and Classical Firsts; and the 1930's, producing four Fellows of Trinity, Cambridge, in as many years and a number of other academics. Such heights have not been scaled since. But the standard of the Commoner entry has probably improved since the last war and, as suggested in the last chapter, the gap between College and Commoner performance has narrowed. Already by 1948 the ground lost during the war years was thought to have been recovered, and with strong competition for all Public School places, the prep school headmasters were complaining that Winchester Entrance was as difficult as winning scholarships to other schools. Through the 1950's and 1960's, with something like one boy in five of all those who left each year winning an award at Oxford or Cambridge, Winchester stood alone on a pinnacle of academic excellence. Since then numerous factors have combined to bring about a levelling effect: the need to increase numbers, the falling birth-rate, high inflation, improved teaching in other schools, the reorganisation of secondary and higher education, and changing social patterns. Winchester still gets better results than any other independent boarding school; but there is now a handful of big urban day schools who do better still since they can be even more selective in their entry.

Winchester could no doubt achieve more high grades and University places each year by concentrating more fiercely and more narrowly on academic achievement. But it could only be at the expense of other things which the school rightly holds as important — the awakening of genuine intellectual interest and excitement, the appreciation of aesthetic values in art, music, and literature; the training and application of physical skills in games and handicrafts; the quest for spiritual contentment; and the development of tolerance, compassion, and responsibility in dealings with one's fellow-men. Without these education is an empty shell, wherein are to be found only a few grains of sterile sand and the sound of a distant sea.

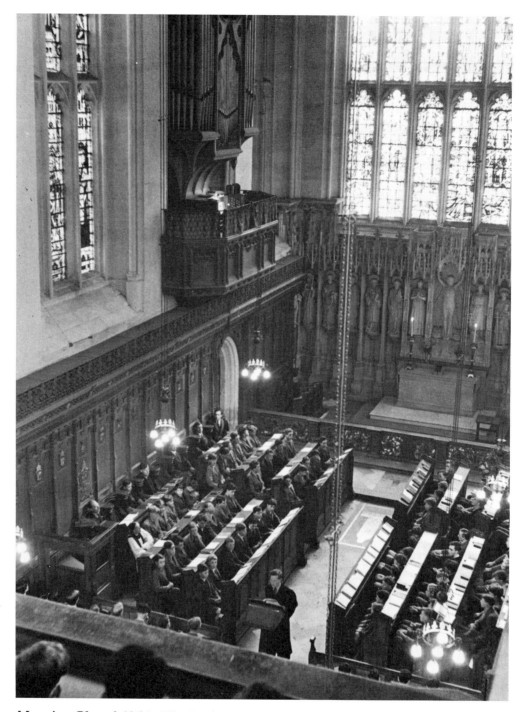

Morning Chapel 1956. The Prefect of Hall, A.B. Swanwick, reading the lesson.

Photograph: Keystone Press

Chapter V

Worship and Belief

The religious attitudes of an institution can hardly be studied in isolation. For in the words of a former chaplain of the College, Budge Firth, "it is a fixed fact that a school is a place where younger citizens are taught by older citizens within a climate of opinion exercising an almost overwhelming power upon them both." The fervour engendered by Arnold's crusade at Rugby in the 1830's was a reflection of the evangelising spirit of the times, just as the agnosticism of many of today's schoolboys is indicative of the bewilderment felt by their parents and teachers. Between these two states lies a tract of history in which the common ground of religious belief was being pared away by a series of divisive forces, such as non-conformity, the Oxford movement, Darwinism, and Freudian psycho-analysis. One effect of this was to polarize religious attitudes among the remaining believers: High Churchmen were set at odds with Low, fundamentalists with evolutionists. But there were many who endeavoured to maintain a central position, by broadening the basis of their beliefs, side-stepping controversy, and eschewing the extremes of opinion on either side.

Latitudinarianism is the imposing name given to this inter-denominational stance. With its emphasis on moral principles rather than doctrinal niceties, and its acceptance of a wide range of ritual observance, it was a form of churchmanship that fitted in well with the ideals of many Public Schools. Headmasters were conscious of the need to keep up the "tone" of their establishments, and parents wanted their children to be improved, as much morally as academically. This could be achieved by a form of Christian education which sought not to impart theological instruction and enrichment of the spiritual part of a boy's nature, but rather to develop his character in accordance with a New Testament ethic of purity, integrity, and compassion. Squire Brown's well-known meditation upon what parting advice he should give to his son Tom suggests that turning out "a brave, helpful, truth-telling Englishman and a gentleman" was how he saw the

Christian aim of Arnold's Rugby; learning to "read his Bible and love and serve God" was something that Tom was expected to do with his mother and nobody else.

If there is, or ever was, such a thing as Public School religion, it would be just this sort of robust, Broad Church Christianity. Certainly the formula evolved in the second half of the 19th century has survived well into our own times, and even in these comparatively godless days Christian ideals of behaviour (rather than dogma) tend to receive emphatic endorsement.

A survey of religious attitudes at Winchester would show the same sort of progression from Evangelicalism to a liberal Broad Churchmanship, and back to today's fragmentation of beliefs. The movement of opinion is expressed partly by the outward form that religious observances take, partly by the declarations that Headmasters and other teachers make. The most important guide is the avowed beliefs of the boys themselves, in so far as these are identifiable.

Even though the College was a monastic foundation with a generous provision of ten priest-fellows and a further trio of chaplains ("hired and removable priests" the statutes call them) to attend to its spiritual functions, the attendance of scholars in Chapel was demanded only on Sundays and holy days. They were excused the endless round of daily services, Matins, Mass and Vespers and the five Canonical Hours, for which senior members might be fined 1d. or 2d. for non-attendance. The Reformation considerably reduced the amount of liturgical worship, but curiously the scholars emerged the worse off for having to rise daily at 5 a.m. in order to attend Chapel. In the course of the next three hundred years only an extra half-hour in bed had been wrung from the authorities, although in winter months the Chapel service was delayed till 6.45. Moberly's concessions in 1862, putting Chapel at 7 a.m. in the summer and 7.30 in the winter, heralded the end of this particular piece of self-mortification. One of Ridding's earliest reforms was the postponement of Morning Chapel until after breakfast. Since 1970 only boys in their first two years have been compelled to attend the weekday morning services. For the rest attendance is voluntary, and therefore minimal.

The Winchester Sunday, so Fearon claimed, was characterised by "the maximum of freedom". This freedom was however tempered by the fact that there were services at 8.00 and 10.30 a.m., and another at 5 p.m. Until 1867 there was also a Scripture lesson at four, and until 1936 boys were not even allowed to change out of their Sunday clothes — which included a top hat. The early morning service was principally for prayer. In mid-morning boys went to the Cathedral for the litany and a sermon. But the

W.A. Fearon, Headmaster 1884-1901, author of 'Sunday Mornings at Winchester'.

main service was Evensong. This had the curious feature of beginning with a sermon, a practice dating from the mid-19th century when the College organist and lay-clerks took part in the Cathedral services as well and could not guarantee that they would get back to chapel in time to play an opening hymn. When Samuel Sebastian Wesley was organist, his limp made him even later, and he would have to stump up the length of the aisle when the sermon was over in order to get to his organ-loft. The custom of the early sermon was preserved until the 1920's, long after the original reason for it had disappeared.

The Cathedral service became an embarrassment. The large number of boys crowded out the other members of the congregation, and compulsory attendance was not conducive to good behaviour. (Let it be remembered that the Cathedral was still outside normal school bounds, so that there was a small element of adventure in getting even this far away from the gates). In 1874 Ridding allowed only senior boys to go, and provided a chapel service for the rest; his successor Fearon in 1890 discontinued regular weekly attendance altogether, and instead arranged that the school should have a service of its own there once a month. This institution of "Cathers" lasted, not without some of the old abuses, for nearly seventy years, until the school population grew so large that it could no longer be fitted into the choir. The severed link was not reforged until 1976 when a special Saturday morning service was arranged with the Dean of Winchester who had himself just become a member of the Governing Body. The experiment has been repeated since, at intervals of a year or more; and as this is one of the very few occasions when the whole school is assembled together, it has retained a fitting dignity and importance.

Further changes in the Sunday timetable were slow in coming. The double dose of sermons was an obvious target. Fearon had introduced some variety by making the morning sermon a lesson in Church history; but this smacked too much of the classroom, and when Burge was appointed Headmaster in 1901 he won instant adoration by abolishing this extra sermon altogether. The compulsory early morning prayer was also abandoned in favour of a voluntary Communion service.

Not until 1959, when the whole issue of compulsory religion was beginning to seethe in the melting-pot, did further modification take place. Over the course of the next ten years liturgical innovations were accompanied by an increasing element of choice; but as these reforms were reflections of the changing patterns of belief, they are best discussed in that context.

––––––––––

When George Moberly entered upon his headmastership, there was more general interest in religious affairs than there had been for a century and a half. The Oxford movement had begun only three years earlier, and Moberly, as a Fellow of Balliol, had been close to the heart of it. He continued to correspond with its leaders, and John Keble was to become a life-long friend when the Moberlys rented a holiday home in his parish of Hursley. The Bishop of Winchester, Charles Sumner, being himself of an evangelical persuasion, was less than welcoming to the new Headmaster whom he suspected of Romish tendencies.

In fact Moberly kept a distance between himself and the new High Church movement. Indeed he deliberately cut himself off from Church affairs, so that for all his eminence he was only occasionally invited to preach outside Winchester. He saw his pastoral role as being limited to the school itself,

A congregation of old and young Wykehamists filling the Cathedral nave for the Quingentenary Service in 1893.

and his ideas in this field were influenced much more by a fellow-headmaster, Thomas Arnold, than by any theologian of the day.

Arnold's approach to school religion was based on the premise that boys living in a community would always tend to lead each other on into wickedness; the only way to curb this unfortunate tendency was to educate the most senior boys in the ways of Christian virtue, and then use them to spread a Christianising influence through the rest of the school. Flogging and expulsion were more direct expedients for keeping the tone of the place wholesome.

Moberly had himself been a scholar at Winchester a few years after Arnold, but did not get to know him until he went to Rugby as an examiner in about 1830. He was immediately impressed by Arnold's reformative work, and when he took over Winchester in 1936 he determined to lead a similar crusade. He too regarded all "assemblages of young boys" as being "endangered by many sorts of evil" and speaks of "this original mass of evil in all schools". The parents, he thought, were chiefly to blame for encouraging their children to idleness and deceitfulness, and "until the earliest training of our boys shall be regulated on a more perfect and Christian model, it is difficult to see by what means this original source and spring of evil in our community can be stopped."

These quotations all come from the preface to his first volume of Sermons, published in 1844. The sermon was one means by which he tried to check the surge of evil; his predecessors had but rarely ventured into the pulpit, and it was the good Warden Barter who had first undertaken to preach regularly at the Sunday afternoon service. But somnolence and distraction are great underminers of the sermon's effectiveness as a means of instruction. Moberly wanted to reach the hearts of his pupils, and the instrument he chose was Confirmation. A generation earlier the sacrament of Holy Communion had been of little significance. It was, it seems, celebrated only three times a year; no-one was expected to attend except the Prefects, and they had to come whether they had been confirmed or not — and in evening dress too. But now Confirmation was made a climactic event in a boy's life. Unaided, and on top of the enormous burden of academic and administrative work which he already carried, Moberly himself undertook a weekly Catechism class for the unconfirmed boys. In the term of Confirmation (which happened at Advent in alternate years) he went through the sacraments in detail with all the sixty or more candidates, and gave each of them two private interviews in his study. The practice of self-examination he particularly urged upon them, so that they should be aware not only of their own failings but of their responsibility to others; for the "Christianising" that he had in mind, though based on spiritual instruction, was above all a form of social discipline. This emphasis is clearly seen in the sort of questions which he bade the College Prefects ask themselves

George Moberly, Headmaster 1836–1866.

in preparation for Holy Communion: "Have I caused any of the Inferior Boys to be late in going into Chapel, and so exposed him to punishment, and to ruffled devotions . . . Have I done anything in their presence which I know is forbidden, such as unlawful drinking, playing cards, behaving noisily or otherwise disorderly at night, etc., etc., and so incurred the double guilt of disobedience in my own person, and of offence to them?"

Religion then was for underpinning the moral conduct of the school, and its development, he thought, set the Public Schools apart from other teaching establishments where authority simply acted as an instrument of repression. Since it was for the good of the whole community as well as the individual, there was a positive duty to instil it into the boys. These two aspects of Moberly's attitude to school religion, the practical and the compulsory, are discussed in the preface to his second volume of Sermons (1848) which treats of Fagging and the role of the Prefect: "It is plain that those who are to hold power must be trained and fitted to use it well. Something must be at work in the school — something very different in kind from a mere system of police . . . something which, first fitting them to obey in a manly, frank, and self-respecting way, may fit them by degrees to use such power as is delegated to them over others . . . It must be a system of practical religion, imparted to the boys throughout the school . . . Make the boys religious, not sentimentally, nor argumentatively, not captiously, not inventively; but catechise them faithfully and painfully, prepare them faithfully for Confirmation . . . take them, as often as you think it proper for such youthful Christians, with specific preparation, to the Holy Communion . . . Carry all this out simply, faithfully and unfalteringly . . . and you need not fear for the general growth of that Christian highmindedness and sense of responsibility in which the system of fagging is to find its security and efficacy. There will grow up a race of modest, earnest, noble-minded youths, in whom the free Public School habits, blended with Church training, have produced just such a character as a father would delight to see in a son, and as fits them for the faithful and high principled discharge of any duties to which they may be called in life."

What effect this had on the generality of boys it is impossible to assess; but it did set a pattern for Public School religion, traces of which can still be seen today. At Winchester the Moberly principles were deliberately perpetuated by one of his brightest pupils, W.A. Fearon, who followed Ridding as Headmaster in 1884. When Fearon was a thirteen year old schoolboy, he was, he said, "already drifting into bad ways". But Confirmation classes brought about his salvation, and for the rest of his long life he manifested a degree of piety and earnestness which would have been most gratifying to his old teacher, and which he tried, with no great success, to transmit to the next generation. Apart from some tinkering with the Sunday services, he simply allowed things to carry on as they were. He continued to oversee the preparation of all Confirmation candidates, but now the larger numbers in the school meant that he could not give the same individual attention as Moberly had done; instead he would set written questions on his talks, and housemasters were expected to correct them, however unfitted or disinclined they might be for this exercise.

Fearon was a conscientious preacher, but his enthusiasm for the minutiae of Church history was not shared by many of his hearers. A standard imitation of one of his lectures on the life of an early saint began "Few of you have been at Megalopolis . . ." This is not to say that Winchester was an irreligious place: the saying of private prayers by one's bedside (a practice which Wordsworth had introduced into College in 1835, to his great personal satisfaction) was still respected, and at least in the classroom Fearon's inspirational force still had its effect. But it remains true that the religious education of the time contained little apart from history, or moral education in a religious context. Fearon inherited from Ridding the notion that the main aim of the school was to make boys "manly" and this extract from one of his sermons shows how much the moral sphere overlapped the spiritual: "Why should we not be a sort of Volunteer White Cross army, pledged to stamp out among ourselves, and, as far as possible, hereafter in the world, all contaminating influences, whether of books or of conversation or of society, to abjure all cynical codes of a lower morality, to have done with all false applications of a so-called schoolboy honour — that our spiritual temple may be one from which whatever is mean or base or unworthy may be banished, in which may be found all truth, all manliness, all purity?"

And here is the comment of someone whose time in the school coincided with the last years of Fearon's rule: "Public-school religion in my time was a queer business that I cannot claim to analyse. It is not quite true, as is sometimes said, that it did not exist; but it is nearly true. Fervent piety, especially if manifested in public, was regarded as only less objectionable than open scoffing, blasphemy, or atheism, all four alike being more or less what we would have called 'bad notions' . . . In their hearts perhaps men were a good deal less pagan than they appeared to be, but to them Christianity was primarily a kind of instinct mixed up with a lot of other instincts such as patriotism . . . love of home, and loyalty to Winchester . . . It was a question of other ideals, passionately held, admirable in themselves, but unconnected with Christianity, monopolising young souls completely undeveloped from a religious point of view."

For this Fearon did not bear sole responsibility; the attitudes cherished were those to be generally found among middle-class church-goers of the time, where religion was above all a duty, and the name of God inspired the same sort of reverence as those of Queen and Empire. But the school compounded the situation in two ways. First of all those whose principal duty it should have been to guide the spiritual development of the young

— the elected chaplains — were in many cases not well fitted to do so. Most had been appointed to the staff for quite other reasons, above all academic distinction, and had little idea of how to approach this most delicate of tasks. There were exceptions, Trant Bramston being the most notable: not only did he have the ability, quite unusual at the time, and certainly not to be found in his fellow-chaplains, to win the confidence of his boys, but he also set out to preach a straightforward Christian Gospel, undiluted by references to Public School Morality and the Imperial Mission.

The second factor was the heavy emphasis placed on the pedagogical elements of religious instruction. With Divinity timetabled as a school subject (and only those subjects which could earn marks were treated with much respect by the venal young), this was not surprising. Nor is it wholly discreditable: a sound knowledge of the liturgy and history of the Church is very desirable in anyone who wishes to call himself a Christian, and it is a just criticism that the school today does *not* provide adequate instruction in these matters. Nevertheless, over-emphasis on this sort of factual material, particularly when it is taught by men who set no particular store by it, leads to the feeling that Divinity is just another academic subject like the rest, and that theological questions are fit matter only for intellectual dispute.

The first half of the twentieth century produced very little change. The traditional forms were maintained, and their effectiveness was never seriously questioned by the authorities; some few boys might be inspired by them, most were at least tolerant, and only a handful were actively antagonistic. There were occasional outbreaks of religious enthusiasm, manifesting itself particularly in the hostility between advocates of High and Low Church practice; and the regular visits from the Portsmouth Missioner (see chapter IX) provided lively witness of Christianity in action, a call to which many responded. But again there is little to suggest that any special care was taken over the spiritual guidance of the young Wykehamist. What was on offer was routinely paraded, and he could take it or leave it.

Monty Rendall was the first layman to be appointed Headmaster in modern times. Though he was concerned to promote a proper spirit of devotion in Chapel and of Christian virtue in daily life, his theological ideas merged mistily with romantic notions of mediaeval chivalry and Renaissance beauty, and did not bear close scrutiny. His pupils in Senior Division learnt to egg him on to expound the more obscure passages in the Pauline epistles. "Ah" he would exclaim, gazing up at the ceiling for inspiration, "there is a great and glorious thought behind this bony bit, and at the proper time and place ah shall not burke it."

Alwyn Williams his successor was, to all who met him, indisputably a great and good man. The barest outlines of his academic and ecclesiastical career show how highly his gifts of mind and character were prized —

The embodiment of Rendall's religious and educational ideals. A triptych that he commissioned from Eleanor Fortescue-Brickdale in 1926. The Knight in Shining Armour is F.N. Huggins, and his Squire P.G.T. Kingsley.

Photograph: E.A. Sollars

a Fellow of All Souls, Headmaster of Winchester at 36, Dean of Christ Church, Bishop of Durham and Winchester, Chairman of the Committee which prepared the New English Bible. Yet these same qualities seemed to raise him to an altogether different plane from the ordinary schoolboy; nor was he much at ease in their company. And though he was a brilliant teacher of History, his sermons were too ponderous for many tastes, as if his natural relish for language and his strong sense of fun were inhibited by the traditions and associations of Chapel.

The Chaplains of the period presented a wide range of contrasts — the weak, the strong, and the eccentric. Hewett the naturalist, with his house full of the sons of landed gentry, and shooting-gaiters visible under his cassock at early service; the precisian David, commander of the O.T.C., whose rhetorical fire was in the course of long service damped by self-doubt; the hellenophile Bather, with an overbearing manner and a resonantly bass voice which did little more than frighten the younger boys in Chantry who were his special care; Quirk, a kindly man of donnish humour and interests, but quite out of touch with the lively and irreverent adolescents who made malicious capital out of his flat toneless voice and his shining hairless dome; McDowall, a biologist of formidable intellectual powers who spent much of his life seeking to reconcile his own religious and scientific beliefs, and found it hard to descend from the rarefied plane at which he conducted his own internal debate to the more ingenuous problems of the schoolboy. His Chapel congregations recorded in wonderment characteristic phrases from his sermons, like "the moonlit radiance of the One-ness" and took delight in the solecisms to which his absent-mindedness made him a constant prey, hardly less than in the mental dexterity with which he extricated himself. Then there was the Munner, W.D. Monro, a large square-cut man, a strict housemaster, not without kindness; though he himself had been a Winchester scholar (renowned at the time for the ferocity of his beating and the distance he could kick a football), India, the country of his birth, had first call on his affections, and his time as a don was only an interval between two spells in the missionary field. He had a wide understanding of oriental languages and religions, but combined this with an aggressive brand of Low Churchmanship which was to some not much more reassuring than his general demeanour.

Such were the chaplains of the first part of the century, and if they were aware that there was any sort of crisis in the spiritual well-being of the community, they did little to show it. But a crisis there was. Neither the fervent Evangelicalism nor the liberal Protestantism of the 19th century was so readily acceptable: scientific and historical research had eroded much of the traditional authority of the Church and the Bible, global war and the subsequent social upheavals had brought disillusion and an upsetting of traditional values, the new study of psychology undermined the ancient concepts of sin and guilt. Christianity was in danger of losing its roots in an increasingly secularised and materialistic world.

There were of course men at Winchester who recognised this. One was Spencer Leeson who was ordained in 1939, four years after becoming Headmaster. In his book *Christian Education* he talks of the danger of reducing religion to something that provided a context for social service — a form of "modernism . . . which encouraged men to hope that they might in some way discover a Christianity without the incarnation." Another was Budge Firth, who was Chaplain from 1931 to 1954. He was particularly aware of the gulf that had opened between the attitudes of his generation (much more to those of his pupils) and the comfortable assumptions which his own teachers thirty years before had enjoyed. For them "Christianity was emptied of much of its definite content, and was largely equated with the standards of the educated Englishman at his best . . .; the real church to them, was the fellowship of men dedicated to the public service. For their own life-work, their school was 'the heavenly city' and its chapel the adequate temple thereof." It was necessary, in his opinion, to seek a new Reformation, to build our faith not upon the quaking foundations of Church tradition and Scriptural authority, but upon the bedrock of "private judgement and of personal feeling and reaction . . . We have now to trust the testimony of the Holy Spirit within, and to rally upon the priesthood of all believers."

He did however maintain that this was consonant with the practice of making regular attendance in Chapel compulsory for all. Indeed it was a matter of pride to him that here was one place in England where the ideal of Anglicanism — that "Church" should be co-terminous with "State" — had not been abandoned.

But the tide of opinion was against him. In the 1950's boys began to make public for the first time their criticisms of the compulsory system, and as the turbulent decade of the sixties began the murmurs of protest rose to a shout. Nor was it only rebellious schoolboys who made the noise.

A committee of Chaplains of Oxford Colleges, concerned at the declining number of communicants among their undergraduates, and at the widespread ignorance of even the fundamental tenets of Christian faith, sent a critical memorandum to the Chairman of the Headmaster's Conference. Compulsory Chapel, they said, "is something entirely out of touch with the rest of the community. Only in Schools (and Borstals) does compulsory worship still go on. In a community where the Church increasingly sees itself as living and witnessing in a non-Christian society, the school blurs the distinction, and the essential element of witness is entirely removed."

The idea of making Chapel voluntary was not a new one. In 1936 Leeson had considered experimenting with it, but had decided not to, partly perhaps because of the general state of ignorance about Christianity that he found in the school, but more because the decision once made would be very hard to reverse.

The principal response to the challenge of the early 1960's was to appoint for the first time a professional Chaplain, that is to say, someone whose main function was not teaching but directing the spiritual life of the school. With his guidance a more coherent plan was devised for teaching Divinity throughout the school, and the form of Chapel worship was substantially altered. There had in fact been a small element of flexibility since 1958 when the Sunday evening service became voluntary, and once a term certain other options were offered including a Sung Eucharist. Now the process was taken further: compulsory Matins alternated with Sundays of choice (one could attend a morning Eucharist, or Evensong); and in the weekday morning services, secular readings were introduced in place of the traditional liturgy. These measures served to "hold the line" without making extravagant concessions. But the issue was still a heated one when John Thorn became Headmaster in 1968. He encouraged the debate, and the upshot of a year's deliberation was the decision taken in January 1970 to make the weekday services voluntary for the upper part of the school. Boys in their first two years still had a compulsory service every day, and for everyone there was an obligation of attendance on Sundays (though sometimes a film or talk is offered instead of a corporate act of worship). The younger boys had their Sunday service in St Michael's church *(Michla)*.

For the godless minority even the need to attend a dozen Sunday Matins a year is an affront, for most others it is tolerable, even enjoyable if the music or the sermon is particularly good; for the committed Christian these compulsory services are unsatisfactory just because everyone else is dragooned into coming, and the religious content is tempered to suit the occasion. That is indicative of the problem that still needs to be resolved. It is not true that the present generation of schoolboys has lost its spiritual consciousness but it does seem to be the case that the institutional services no longer meet their needs. When weekday services first became voluntary, 75% of all boys said that they would attend at least occasionally; in fact only the merest handful now do so.

The results of three surveys of religious opinion among the boys (1964, 1969, 1979) give the clearest indication of the way things have been going. Outward conformity has been on the increase, with fewer opposed outright to the idea of compulsory attendance, and more being confirmed. Informal religious services such as an evening Communion in the Chaplain's house may be well attended; and the growing popularity of Divinity A level shows that among some at least there is a good deal of intellectual interest in religious matters. But at the same time the tide of faith is on the ebb. A much smaller proportion would regard it as important to make their Communion regularly or even admit to a belief in God. Ignorance and uncertainty are made worse by indifference. These attitudes are only a reflection of more generally held views in an agnostic and materialist age. It is understandable that fewer of the teaching staff these days should profess much commitment to Christian worship, but it does not make it any easier to convince our pupils of the importance of spiritual values in life.

The response of the school authorities, prompted by a succession of admirable Chaplains such as Paul Bates and David Conner, has been to keep up a programme of religious education through the weekday morning services and through the curriculum; and to try and give every individual some way of finding his God, through a mixture of traditional and informal worship, in both compulsory and voluntary services, through the motets of Tallis and Byrd, the prayerbook of Cranmer, Series 3, devotional meditation, Bible study groups or whatever.

Many pre-1970 Wykehamists would tell you that the service that meant most to them was the one on Saturday evening, when the processional psalm "I was glad" and the great Anglican hymns were thundered out with uninhibited passion. It was a corporate devotional act of the kind that only a school can make, and it gave you a warm feeling inside that some would call a spiritual experience. But truly the religious element in the service was, to adapt Matthew Arnold's dictum, little more than emotion tinged with morality. Therein lies the dilemma: the symbolic rituals of the Church are what the school with its musical, architectural, and intellectual riches, can display in their finest form; but very few schoolboys now seem able to relate these services to an idea of God, or even to find in them a means of seeking Him. So the debate goes on.

Rules of Winchester Football: "The ground is to be good level turf . . ."
Photograph: E.A. Sollars

Chapter VI

Games, Sport and Exercise

The first ten years of the life of Marlborough College were characterised by vandalism, brutality, and finally open rebellion. When G.E.L. Cotton, newly appointed Headmaster in 1852, sought to win a measure of co-operation from his undisciplined pupils by encouraging the development of organised games, he set in motion a process which has had more far-reaching effects than any other aspects of Public School life. From here can be traced the origins of most codes of football played all around the world; from here too came the attitudes that underlay the spirit of English Amateurism and even the ideals of the renascent Olympic movement. At the opening ceremony of the 1896 Athens games, it was fittingly an Englishman — and a Wykehamist — who delivered the Greek ode of welcome: for good measure he later competed in the discus.

Cotton's immediate aim was disciplinary, and he did not at first promote the view that games had much higher educational, let alone moral, purpose. He maintained for instance that "immoderate interest in mere amusement is inconsistent with the sober spirit of watching unto prayer". But no such appeals to godliness could stem the impetus of the games-cult he had unleashed; and since what could not be resisted had to be justified, he was driven to concede that virtue could be found in bodily as well as intellectual excellence "when they are a reflection of moral and religious goodness, when they teach us unselfishness, right principles and justice." The concept of athleticism was born.

In the last quarter of the 19th century this idea of a link between moral excellence and athletic prowess took a firm hold in the Public Schools. Boys under the constraint of academic discipline and monastic living conditions needed little encouragement to project their rivalries onto the games-field. When this competitive spirit was further inflamed by masters who preached a gospel of athleticism, the results could be grotesque. Stories are told of Sherborne's Headmaster at this time, the Reverend F.B. Westcott, who, fired with the same earnestness as his eminent theologian father, would run up and down the touchline screaming exhortations in Latin and Greek, or leap into the fray himself and whack at the laggards with his stick. Even progressive men like F.W. Farrar (housemaster at Harrow, and Master of Marlborough 1871-76) who had himself no regard at all for athletic prowess, were so far taken in thrall by the new philosophy as to talk in these terms: "No-one can make a first rate cricketer if he is not ready and steady and quick and bold . . . You want the very same good qualities in the great cricket-field of life."

Winchester has never in the last two centuries had a Headmaster likely to think of sport in such terms. It is true that when George Moberly was at Oxford he was quite prominent in cricketing circles; when he became Headmaster in 1836 he found himself in the company of a Warden, Robert Barter, whose robust vigour became legendary (he was reported to hit cricket balls into Kingsgate Street from the middle of Meads — a carry of well over 100 yards); and his Second Master, Charles Wordsworth, had represented Oxford in the first rowing and cricket contests against Cambridge. This formidable sporting triumvirate could have made Winchester a school of athletes. They certainly did encourage the growth of organised games. But the dominant values of the school were always Moberly's, and he never compromised his firm belief in the virtues of piety and classical learning. For him, "An idle boy is a boy who loves cricket and so on."

Monty Rendall also had a distinguished sporting career, playing as goalkeeper in the Cambridge soccer XI for two years, then for the Corinthians. His large frame and indifference to physical discomfort were obvious assets in a position much less protected by referees than nowadays. People even talked of him as a possible England player. The idea never seriously attracted him, though in later years he recalled his sporting past with some satisfaction: "Of course when ah was at Cambridge, ah was in with all the greatest and best men of me day; ah knew *all* the Blues. Ah was THE Corinthian. When they wanted a goal-keeper for one of these touring-teams, they sent for ME, ah, for me." When he was Headmaster he manifested a happy indifference to the games his pupils played, gleefully muddling the names of the cups, the names of the players, and even the names of the games themselves. Much of this was pure mischief of course; more significant of his attitude is the fact that he made no mention of athletic achievements in his annual reports to the Governing Body.

The headmasters of the next fifty years could none of them really be called athletic. Alwyn Williams (1924-1935) would, in his younger days, occasionally join in and "bumble around" on the football field, or coach a four on the river; and even in his eighties his gigantic walking stride would cover ground at a speed that left ordinary mortals trailing. His four successors would have been content to trail, I think.

Lords XI of 1860, when Eton won a close game by 19 runs.

It would however be wrong to suggest that Winchester had ever had a priggish attitude towards sport. In the eyes of the boys at any rate, the status of rival schools has always been determined at least in part by their sporting achievements. So Winchester itself succumbed to the pressures of athleticism: games became accepted as part of the curriculum, which meant that men who could play games were attracted onto the staff. Pre-eminent among such people, in recent memory, are: Rockley Wilson, who played cricket for Yorkshire and England (when he applied for leave of absence to tour Australia in 1920-21, Monty Rendall spoke of him as "one of two or three 'gentlemen' only who are responsible for the tone of the visiting team"); Harry Altham, who crowned a life devoted to cricket by becoming President of the M.C.C.; and Hubert Doggart, also M.C.C. President and Treasurer, who represented Cambridge at five different sports, and played cricket for England. Fine sportsmen all, but primarily teachers; and they all had good University degrees.

Again though Winchester has never professed to be principally a sporting school, its athletic record for much of this century has overall been the equal of its rivals. During the years 1920-1960 for instance, the school won most of its cricket matches (despite a spell of twenty years without a success against Eton), and provided more cricket Blues at Oxford and Cambridge than any other school; in the six years 1955-60 only one school game was lost, and that by one run on the last ball; the soccer teams of 1925-28 won all their school matches and led the way to consecutive victories in the Arthur Dunn Cup (for Public School Old Boys) in 1929-31; there were also more soccer Blues in 1919-1948 than from any other school. Winchester rowing, limited by the narrowness of the Itchen navigation canal, did not produce an VIII until 1939 (winning the Princess Elizabeth Cup at Henley in 1949 and 1954), but won the competition for School IV's at Marlow nine times in between 1924 and 1939; "Princes" (the school rackets pair) won the Public School doubles ten times between 1929 and 1959, with

Winchester Cricketers in Hunter Tent, Eton March 1963: (Left to right) N. Craig, V. Awdry, F. Hibbert, D. Pilbrow, P. Scott, Harry Altham, N. Sinker, 'Podge' Brodhurst (Master in charge), Vince Broderick (Professional).

Photograph: E.A. Sollars

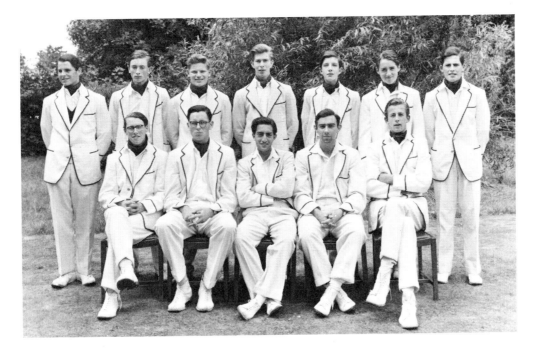

Lords XI 1959, Winchester's strongest post-war side: (Back row, left to right) J. Sanders, G. Daniels, N. Majendie, J. Travis, R. Thomas, J. Townsend, C. Snell; (seated left to right) C. Dinwiddy, R. Jefferson, Nawab of Pataudi, J. Patrick, R. Watson. Half of them went on to play First Class cricket, and Pataudi was captain of India. Photograph: E.A. Sollars

three consecutive victories in 1943-5 and again in 1949-51. For good measure we should add the inter-school trophies won for fives (1931), golf (1954), skiing (1935, 1956), sailing (1958) and shooting (winners of the Ashburton Shield in 1919, 1930, 1937, 1955).

Quite a number of Wykehamists have gone on to win distinction as games-players in later life: Douglas Jardine, captain of England cricket in the "body-line" era; Max Woosnam and Claude Ashton, two of the last amateurs to captain the full English international XI at soccer; John Emrys Lloyd, who represented the country for Fencing in all the Olympics from 1932 to 1952, and would surely have won gold medals but for the war; the Nawab of Pataudi, cricket captain of India even after losing his sight in one eye; and recently Howard Angus, a uniquely successful amateur in the princely games of rackets (World Champion 1973-5) and Real Tennis (World Champion 1976-81).

In the last twenty years success has been harder to come by. The increase in competition provides some explanation: there are now far more schools trying to get their names on the honours boards so long dominated by a handful. But much of the responsibility lies with changes of attitude and emphasis within the school. To understand that, we must go back to the beginning again.

———————

For much of the 19th century the boys devised and organised their own games. Instances of help and encouragement from the teaching staff did sometimes occur: when Charles Wordsworth became Second Master in 1835, he brought a four-oared boat from Oxford to teach some rowing (but on Leave-out days only), he helped to prepare proper turf for cricket in Meads, and he brought about a significant change in the playing of Winchester Football (see p.106). But these were exceptions. The boys played their cricket and football when and where they could, used the backs of buildings for rackets and fives, swam in the lock at 'First Pot' and ran races round Meads. Prize money and trophies were often donated privately; the administrative expenses were paid from annual subscriptions of about a pound per boy.

As in many other aspects of school life, a significant change came with the accession of George Ridding to the headmastership in 1867. He greatly increased the facilities by promoting the construction of a new Rackets Court (1871), Gymnasium (1878) and three new Fives Courts (1882 — the earlier courts were the gift of his father in 1862). The institution of a proper Boat Club dates from the beginning of his rule. He also appointed to his staff a number of men with sporting interests: A.J. Toye, the first Winchester don to involve himself in coaching cricket, and one of the best fives players of his time; E.J. Turner, a masterly lob-bowler; T. Kensington, the first rowing coach; and J.A. Fort, who throughout his long teaching career never lost his boyish enthusiasm for cricket and football. Furthermore, although the boys continued to administer the finances of all their games for the rest of the century, the school provided regular subventions to help pay for professional bowlers in the cricket nets, and major expenses like relaying the turf or purchasing chairs for spectators.

The boys had never needed much urging to take their games more seriously. The early numbers of *The Wykehamist* contain page after page of sporting journalism, reaching a climax every June when Eton Match offered a wealth of opportunities for learned prognostication, graphic description, and morbid analysis. For many boys, the games were more important than anything else they did at school. In such an atmosphere it was even possible to publish a suggestion that the beautiful 17th century College Sick House should be pulled down for the sake of enlarging the cricket ground.

Eton Match at Winchester, 1902. Eton made 63 in this innings; but Winchester had only managed 54 (Sandeman 10 for 22), and lost by four wickets.

In spite of this there was persistent hostility to the idea of taking the direction of games out of boys' hands and making them more professional. Certainly sport in the school was becoming increasingly competitive. The new facilities and the reorganisation of Commoners inevitably led to the birth of house-competitions. The first inter-house cup was given for rowing in 1873, and other sports soon followed. The acquisition of silver trophies for the sideboard became a means of measuring the status of a house. But there were limits. An editorial in *The Wykehamist* of June 1875 deploring "the present professional mania" attracted no protesting voices, at a time when the correspondence columns were full of vigorous controversy. The writer congratulated the school on being the only one not to have a professional for its rackets, but lamented that "Winchester is nevertheless tainted by the prevailing contagion: we too make cricket a task instead of a pastime". Soon, he prophesied, public opinion would turn against professionalism, and "what school should then take the lead in such a movement, if not Winchester, which has lately won leadership in intellectual pursuits . . . and can well leave to others, for a time, the superiority in merely physical exercise?"

During the last twenty years of the century remarkably few vigorous young men were recruited to the staff. Towards the end of Fearon's headmastership (1901) the average age of the dons was around fifty, and a gaunt and grizzled lot they look in the photographs. Not surprisingly they had lost most of their interest in games — except for the indefatigable Fort, who would rush into print with Notes on batting and fielding and kicking and running whenever his critical eye detected signs of sloppiness or technical deficiency in the young.

But if official interest was limited, the general movement was towards more and more competitive games. In the 1890's soccer was established to provide football matches against other schools; the School IV took on more rowing opponents, and beat them; there were new rackets fixtures and fives matches; and cricket received further impetus from its best ever decade, with four wins over Eton. Domestic competitions proliferated too, and regular exercise, listed on a boy's weekly Ekker Roll, became compulsory.

Another *Wykehamist* editorial (June 1893) addressed itself to the subject of athleticism: ". . . the fact is that our games have become too much of a business to be satisfied with anything but our undivided attention. Cricket and football have become specialized. No doubt the effect has been to raise the standard of play, but we doubt whether increase of skill brings with it increase of pleasure." Protesting voices like that are to be heard in one generation after another. Even though the fixture lists got more and more crowded, and athletic competition increasingly became the focus for House Spirit, Philistia could never claim outright victory. While the institution of compulsory games was accepted as an unalterable tenet of school life,

Dons Common Room at the time of Fearon's departure in 1901. Back row (left to right): Garbutt, Fort, Buckland, E.D.A. Morshead, Macdonald, W.P. Smith, Cruickshank, Steel, F. Morshead, Cook, Bell, Furley; (Middle row) Hewett, Bramston, Wrench, Rendall, Fearon, Griffith, Kensington, Turner, Godfrey; (Front row) R.K. Parr, David, Bather, Hardy, Du Pontet, Irving.

and the most trivial details of athletic performances were thought fit matter for publication in the school magazines (indeed new magazines were regularly started in order to extend the sports coverage), yet serious debate was still possible about whether Boat Club should be abolished in the interest of war-time economy, whether the Racket Courts should be demolished, whether Winchester Football should be abandoned, whether the school's intellectual and cultural societies should not be given more encouragement at the expense of games, and so on.

With this freedom of opinion came a good deal of freedom of action. Whatever the preference for forms of exercise that redounded to "the glory of the House" there was no bar to the foundation of societies and clubs whose aims were purely recreational: golf (1891), squash (1892), chess (1899), hockey (1902). Fishing on the Itchen and its tributaries in Water Meads had long been a favourite summer pastime, and a proper club was started in 1910. Sailing on the Hamble river was authorised from around 1930. Tennis courts were built in 1933.

So though it might have been considered almost treasonable not to watch Eton Match, though senior house cricket matches were fought to the death for days on end (over 1250 runs were amassed in one such final: by contrast one junior side was dismissed for a single run — a bye), though "pot-hunting" was a major preoccupation for many boys and some housemasters, yet there was tolerance of the non-athletic, respect for choice of recreation, and furthermore excessive keenness was liable to be branded by the strongly pejorative term "heartiness".

If the school still gives the impression of being games-dominated in this period (up until the late 1950's), reflecting the prevailing ethos of the time, it was assuredly much less so than other schools. Cultural activities were steadily developing at the same time (as will be seen in the next chapter), and official support for them ensured that they would always receive a proper measure of respect.

During the last twenty years, ideas about the function of exercise and team-games in schools have had to be modified. Some of the pressures have come from inside (i.e. from what the boys would or would not do), others from outside. Two of the most important external factors have been the intensification of training for competitive sports up and down the country, and the increased importance attached to fitness for reasons of health. "Amateurish" is now a term of disdain almost, and there is no longer a place in international teams for the effortless "brilliance" of John Buchan heroes whose only training consists of a scamper over the Scottish grouse-moors in pursuit of blackguards. Now the Olympic athlete begins his preparation three years before the Games: the executive cycles to work and jogs around the park on Sundays.

At the time when these new ideas began to permeate the ancient

Coxed Fours on the river: (above) by the old boathouse (1903), (below) at the finishing line (1964).

fastnesses, the monolith of authoritarianism was already beginning to crumble; traditional attitudes to games were more urgently questioned, and changes were not long in coming. An early pointer was the formation in 1957 of a Croquet Club whose avowedly anti-athletic philosophy was signalised by having a tie only fractionally different from the august colours of the Old Wykehamist Cricket Cub; great was the umbrage taken in certain circles. Rumblings against the Great School Compulsories (Chapel, Corps, and Games) sounded with increasing vehemence in the early 1960's. Cuts were made in the extent of some of the house competitions; Senior Steeplechase was made voluntary after a series of discreditable episodes — competitors taking lifts or short-cuts, and in 1961 the ultimate cavalier gesture when one covered the course on horse-back. But besides the protests a new and positive philosophy was emerging too, suggesting that playing was for fun and for exercise and only incidentally for glory. Conflicting views, traditional and modern, were encapsulated in *The Wykehamist* in a vigorous debate about whether "if a thing is worth doing, it is worth doing badly". The College Tutor said it was, the Old Wykehamist said it wasn't.

Bright symbol of the new age was the Physical Education complex, opened with considerable misgivings in 1969. How very un-Wykehamical it seemed! Instead of the turbid and chilly waters of the Itchen which, with few embellishments, had served the naked bathers of the school for a hundred years (swimming trunks were another concession to modernity hard won in the 1960's), here was an architectural showpiece, a pool of limpid turquoise framed by glistening tiles in steamy sub-tropical warmth; instead of the old Victorian drill-hall where club-swingers, gymnasts, boxers, fencers and weight-lifters trod on each others' toes, and stirred up evocative odours compounded of dust, sweat, coconut-matting, leather and embrocation, here was a spotless gymnasium the size of an aircraft hangar, with the finest Olympic apparatus, and a multi-coloured tracery of lines on the floor to mark courts for badminton, volleyball and basketball; here was no mere fencing gallery, but a *salle*, electrically rigged; here was a separate gym, just for weight-training, and ropes in neatly disciplined coils for use on the climbing wall; here were changing rooms for men, and for *women*. Good heavens, did they mean to go co-educational or something?

If the new temple of sport took some getting used to (the title "Ekker Mecca" was too good to last; with predictable dullness it reverted to "P.E. Centre"), then so did its new votary. For the second time in the school's history the name G. Dyson was to be associated with new initiatives and changes of attitude. Enormously distinguished in his own field (one-time chief national coach to the A.A.A.), he came fresh to a Public School environment, and looked for ways of blending the traditional values with modern thinking on the role of exercise. This is how he summed up his views: "We should attempt to inculcate not merely an aspiration for better

The technology of fitness. J. Elliott in the P.E. Centre using a bicycle ergometer; the instrument right of centre is for measuring the pulse-rate.

Photograph: T. Wilson

performance in this or that sport, but an attitude towards fitness and physical recreation in general which will persist and motivate when, perhaps, interest in a particular activity wanes. And this can be achieved without threatening valued academic standards (indeed these could benefit): without pursuing the ideal of *citius, altius, fortius* to the ultimate elimination of both education and play".

A logical corollary of this argument was that physical exercise should remain compulsory (with the freedom to choose any sport you liked). But this ran counter to the spirit of the times: the new liberalism included the freedom to choose *not* to play any games. So the amount of compulsion became for most boys small, for senior ones negligible. Even a boy capable of representing the school could decide that he did not want to, and stick to his decision with a good conscience. For a time cricket waned: sailing flourished.

The decades of the 1970's and 1980's have seen a further erosion, slow but perceptible, of the edifice of house competition. What is perhaps surprising is that the principal reason has not been indifference, rather the increased attention being paid to school teams. Rising standards in football and rowing, for instance, throughout the country's schools make all competitors train more strenuously. The best athletes of one age-group may now expect to play matches together as a team at every level from their first year to their last: the serious rowers have to find time for rigorous training schedules and regattas which eat into their working hours as well as their leisure. Not for the first time there is a problem of balance, and with increased pressure on all fronts the modern schoolboy cannot, like his ancestors, "proceed as if life were one long game of cricket". But even if parents have long ceased to send their children to Public Schools to absorb the physical and moral lessons of compulsory team-games, it is still a time and a place where something of educational value can be gained from competition, the development of athletic skills, and the habit of exercise.

In any account of sport at Winchester, space must be found for those games which are indigenous to it. *The Oxford Companion to Sports and Games* has articles on Winchester Fives and Winchester Football. The fives, played with gloved hands, is really just a compromise between the Eton version (with a host of curious obstacles in the court) and the Rugby one (played in a plain rectangular box). The Winchester court has just one small buttress in the left-hand wall, which adds a nice variety to the rallies. This peculiarity is at least as old as the 1882 courts, and has proved attractive enough to be copied in about a dozen other places in the country. But the present courts (1909) are now used as much by outside organisations as by boys in the school; one has even been transformed into a store for theatrical flats. The world of fives is a shadowy one, but the light glimmers strongly enough for there to be no immediate fear of extinction.

Of Winchester Football there is more to be said, particularly because of the bearing it has on the issues raised in the first half of the chapter.

With the eye of faith the origins of the game may be traced back to the 17th century or earlier — wherever in fact reference is made among the exiguous sources to boys kicking footballs around. But for an understanding of its peculiarities the only important historical fact is that it was first played on the flat space at the top of St. Catherine's Hill. It was originally little more than a free-for-all whose aim was simply to propel the ball over the opponents' line. Junior boys, marshalled down each side of the pitch, kept the ball in play and stopped it rolling down the slopes of the hill or getting lost in the trees.

When the first rules were introduced we do not know; perhaps a little after 1790 when the scholars were allowed the use of Meads as a playing field. At any rate by 1825 or so the game had a recognisable form, and matches were being played between College and Commoners. There were 22 on each side, 20 of them in the scrimmage or *hot*, and the other two as *behinds*. The *hot* formed at the beginning of the game sometimes lasted throughout the entire match . There is a story of dubious authenticity about a Commoner who lingered behind on the field of play after the match was over: he wanted to reassure himself that there really was a ball on the pitch, as he had not once set eyes on it during the actual game.

In the middle of the goal-line (called *worms*) two scholars' gowns or coats were placed a few feet apart. Between them the goal-keeper (*last behind*) stood with feet apart. Incongruously he also acted as referee. If the ball was forced over *worms*, but on either side of the goal, it counted as one point (a *shit* — normal Wykehamical corruption of the word "shot" — or more decorously *schitt*); if over the gowns, but untouched by the *last behind*, it scored two (a *gowner*); if through his legs or over his head, three (a *goaler*). The by-standers were also integrated into the game as *kickers-in*, propelling the ball in the direction required by the team they favoured; but in order to prevent too much encroachment they were kept behind a rope on either side of the pitch.

At the same time there was developed for less formal contests a kicking game (called *Long Game*) without any *hots*, and with fewer players cluttering up the pitch. This was the parent of the six-a-side game (VI's) still played today, where long kicking and hard running, the principal features, make for fast and spectacular action. The 22-a-side contest has been abandoned (except for an annual charade when the best two players in College take on the junior XXII); now XV's and X's are played, which combine elements of the old *hotting* and kicking games. The form of the game is still evolving (the rule-book is now in its thirteenth edition), and though many traditional features are still recognisable it has progressed a long way from the time when even seasoned veterans of the Peninsular War would pale at the sight of the *hots* converging.

In 1843 the Second Master, Charles Wordsworth, the first Winchester don to take a real interest in the boys' games, brought about an end to the miseries of compulsory *kicking-in*. From the following year the lines of shivering juniors down each side of the pitch were replaced by canvas screens. The ropes were retained, to keep the players from charging into them; but in other ways the screens were doubly unsatisfactory — they were difficult to keep upright, and impossible for spectators. So the big matches between College and Commoners continued to be played without screens (but still between ropes), until in 1866 lengths of netting, suspended on iron frames, were introduced for the side-lines. The ropes were not really needed now, but had to be retained as they had become absorbed into the strategy of the game. The area between them and the *canvas* (as the netting continued to be called) now formed a sort of no-man's land where the ball could be held defensively by forming a *hot* round it. Sometimes such a *hot on ropes* could last twenty minutes or more. It took careful legislation, and the use of winches for tightening the ropes, to open the game out again.

A 'hot' in a 22-a-side game, as played in the 1830's. Illustration from R.B. Mansfield: School Life at Winchester College (1866).

A drawing by Richard Baigent (1838) showing a game of Winchester Football being played on Commoner Field, with rows of 'kickers-in' down each side of the pitch.

The complicated apparatus and the ritualistic appearance of some of the play does make the game seem very odd to anyone who does not know it, and amazement is expressed at its survival into the 1980's. In fact its future is less in question than it has been many times in the past. The reasons are worth investigation.

In the mid-19th century there were of course no standard rules for football. The game at Winchester took its form from the peculiar circumstances of its origins described above. The kinds played at other schools also had their own individual features, reflecting the influence of topography, tradition or mere chance. In 1846 an amalgamation of Salopians and Etonians brought about the foundation of the Cambridge Football Club, and the Cambridge Rules published two years later by a committee which included a Wykehamist were the first to be widely accepted. In October 1863 a decisive move was made among the London Clubs to achieve uniformity: the Football Association was formed and further meetings planned with the intention of framing a single universal code, to encompass both the kicking and the handling games. As a first step the Secretary, from Barnes Club, wrote round to all footballing schools to invite their cooperation. But parochialism prevailed. The schools did not want to be amalgamated, and Winchester pointedly demonstrated its independence by undertaking the first codification of rules for its own game; they were published a month later, at almost exactly the same time as the first draft of Association rules was being discussed.

So Winchester cut itself off from the mainstream of English football, and had to be content with domestic competition until soccer was accepted as an additional winter game (the first official school match was against Charterhouse in 1902). In the early days there were attempts to spread the Winchester game. A *canvas* was erected yearly in the Parks at Oxford between 1866 and 1873, and some non-Wykehamists took up the game. Let it be known to posterity that in the final match a team of former scholars defeated the Rest of the World by 13 goals to 7. At about the same time the Principal of the Diocesan College at Rondebosch, the Reverend G. Ogilvie, was managing to popularise the game in South Africa. In fact Winchester football was the dominant code in the Cape Colony until 1878 when it was supplanted by Rugby. Changes in the Rugby rules at about this time, particularly the reduction of numbers from twenty to fifteen in a team, and the development of running and passing tactics, made it a more obviously attractive game — and it had no need of the paraphernalia of ropes, posts, netting and iron stanchions. So the Winchester game was pruned back to the parent stock, and has remained firmly rooted in the flinty soil of Meads ever since.

It is true there have been times when the future of the game was in doubt. In the very early days when the rising number of Commoners meant that College could no longer hold its own, one writer in *The Wykehamist*

Houses XV, 1870 – before the present brown and white stripes were adopted as colours.

suggested that the time had come to adopt the new Association rules instead. But the force of conservatism prevailed — in spite of producing one of the feeblest arguments and most misguided observations of the decade: "Few people are now of the opinion that (Association) Football will come to be a universal game. The Association rules are losing ground, nor is there much to recommend itself in them."

Abolitionists have continued to make themselves heard from time to time since then. Rugby football has often been suggested as an alternative: one or two experimental games were played in the 1870's against local clubs, and there was a flurry of interest in the 1920's when Ian Smith had, in a matter of two or three years, graduated from Commoner VI to an Oxford Blue to a Scottish International Cap. Since 1954 rugger has been played intermittently by enthusiasts in the school, with the cooperation if not the active encouragement of the authorities.

From a logical and practical point of view there have always been plenty of reasons why Winchester Football should be abolished in favour of one of the national games. What helped to save it in the past was the stock of moral virtues associated with it. Since there is no dribbling allowed in the Winchester rules, the player has to kick the ball as hard as he can, then run after it and try to charge down his opponent's kick. The act of charging down, picturesquely called *raising a plant*, requires a person to run straight at the kicker in the full knowledge that a heavy wet leather ball may be propelled hard into his face or stomach or — worse. If he does succeed in getting a rebound by this means, he wins a material advantage for his side and cheers from the spectators. But to court such personal discomfort deliberately on the football field requires a certain reckless courage and an inversion of the normal scale of values which places personal survival above scoring goals. To our ancestors such manifestations of "manliness" appeared wholly admirable, indeed something to be cultivated. It was as if football had been specifically designed to fulfil an educational need. "The true Winchester game surpasses all others for testing the pluck, skill and endurance of its votaries" wrote *The Wykehamist* proudly. This combination of qualities was just what a chap needed if he was going out to face a crowd of rioting natives in the streets of Peshawar, or leading his company at a steady pace into the machine-guns of Beaumont Hamel.

It may seem absurd to equate the affrays of the football field with actions where men endanger and even sacrifice their lives: it would certainly be in the highest degree improper for me, belonging as I do to a post-war generation, to question or belittle the convictions of such men. But there is evidence to show that, whether it actually had any effect on their later behaviour or not, many boys did accept from their teachers the notion that Winchester Football was a good preparation for the dangers that might face them in life.

George Leigh Mallory was something of a Wykehamical paragon, a scholar as well as an athlete, universally liked and admired. He was soon to make a name, and later a legend for himself by his mountaineering achievements, culminating on June 8th 1924 when he and Sandy Irvine were "lost to human sight between heaven and earth" when "going strong for the top" of Mount Everest. By nature given to introspection, he was led by his first experiences as a Gunnery Officer on the Western Front in 1916 to examine his personal courage. He wrote to his wife: "Curious how I have found myself going back for reassurances to old football days at Winchester! I have found myself repeating words from one of the little red volumes of Artillery Training — 'such a complete absence of self-interest that he will do his duty in the hour of danger coolly and accurately".

These sentiments were not just a personal foible. They echo the lines of a poem to a Wykehamist who died in the Boer War; it ends

> Old School, if thou hast still
>   Such hearts remaining,
> It has not served thee ill —
>   The old football training!

A game of VI's being played on Meads (1972).
Photograph: Simon Abrahams

> And England shall not lack
> Sons to defend her
> Like him who shouted back
> That "No surrender!"

Even in 1941 General Wavell was receiving telegrams of congratulations for "hotting the enemy over worms".

The following story will serve to reinforce the suggestion that teachers deliberately encouraged this attitude towards football.

Some of the boys who came to Winchester in the wake of the Great War could not help a feeling of inadequacy. How could they possibly measure up to the heroism of their predecessors who had fought and died, whose names and exploits were constantly held up as an example, whose memorial was taking visible shape and daily absorbing more and more of the Headmaster's attention? The Second Master, Monty Wright (who as a boy had been in College with George Mallory) had fought through the War in the Coldstream Guards: he had been wounded and won the M.C. and

Bar. His answer to the self-doubters was this (and entirely characteristic of him): he would have them believe that it required the same order of bravery to go straight for a "plant" as to go into battle. Nobody scoffed. Again, when the anti-Winchester-Football lobby was making itself heard in 1926, he published a lengthy defence in *The Wykehamist*: after long and varied experience (he had also taught at Eton) he had concluded that of all football codes, Winchester's was "the best for the average games-player . . . The moderate player, provided he goes hard and goes straight, gets plenty of opportunities in our game, and the game affords him the best possible training in body and soul. There is no place in it for the shirker."

Such sentiments are not much in favour today. The modern Wykehamist rejects the idea that the playing of games constitutes a valuable training in moral qualities. "It is very doubtful whether learning to 'raise a plant' without flinching teaches you to do anything except raise more plants" he writes (1970). Winchester Football must therefore find its justification elsewhere.

It would be tedious to rehearse all the arguments currently used for and against its continuance. There can certainly be no agreement. Some regard its peculiarities as an absurd anachronism, even a damaging manifestation of exclusiveness; others see them as a protection against the competitive pressures which take the fun out of sporting fixtures against other schools. Some players revel in the mud-larking to which the game inevitably degenerates midseason; others abhor it. But the most important fact is that most people enjoy it: it is usually fun to play, even for the non-athletic, and can be very exciting to watch. It needs no further justification. If any were required, a visit to Meads to experience the tingling atmosphere of a XV's or VI's match would be enough.

Like many of Winchester's institutions, it is inconceivable that anyone should invent or introduce such a game today; but because it is there already, and because with every passing year of its existence there is less reason to abandon it, so it will continue — a source of bewilderment to foreigners, anxiety to sensitive mothers, and rampant nostalgia to Wykehamist fathers.

Experts conferring. 'Jacker' after watching his last game of VI's, with the Houses Captain, I.G. Bentley (1972).

Photograph: Simon Abrahams

Photograph: T. Wilson

Workers with metal (above) and clay (below)

Photograph: A. Spokes

Chapter VII

Arts and Pastimes

To a small boy newly liberated from the restraints of preparatory school routine, the hours of spare time in the Winchester day are at first rather daunting. Here no bells ring to tell him to stop one activity and start another; no master-on-duty sends him spinning from pillar to post with a genial cuff over the head. The day — or half of it — is his. The work in the lower part of the school does not occupy more than his hours "up to books" and his "toytime": the games commitment is, in most cases, undemanding. He is left with at least twenty hours in the week to fill as he pleases. What can he do?

If he is a practising musician, then there is no difficulty. He can receive tuition on any one (or more) of sixteen different instruments: he can sing in the choir for Chapel or Michla; he can be a member of Glee Club (choral society). And some sort of concert (most of them free of charge) will be there for him to enjoy just about every week. If he prefers the visual arts, he can go to the spacious new Art School and learn about *gouache* and *collage* and "reserved lights". If he likes using his hands, he can throw pots, carve in wood or mould in clay. For the carpenter there is a wondrous array of machinery, expertise and geniality in "Mill" where design and Technical Graphics receive as much emphasis as the traditional crafts: for the electronics enthusiast a new Projects Laboratory next to the main Computer centre; for the engineer, a metal workshop and Vehicle Maintenance sheds where you can make your own car or hovercraft. There is a room for book-binding, several more for photography, and half a floor occupied by the Printing Society.

So long as his interests can be regarded as wholesome and in some sense educational, there is likely to be a Society that caters for them. Leaders in the field, by virtue of antiquity, are those for Natural History, Debating, and Archaeology; among the newest is Rock and Pot (for climbers and cavers I should explain). In between come Bell Ringing, Science, Chess, Stamps, Films and Gramophone Records.

Of course he may decide that his talents are histrionic, and as there are anything up to eight or ten plays performed a year, it should not be long before he sees his name in print on a programme; and if he never graduates beyond Third Messenger, there are more opportunities open to him as a technician — in lighting, set-construction, stage-management and make-up.

The status of these different activities varies enormously. Some of them have become part — a small part admittedly — of the regular curriculum at the bottom of the school; some have instructors on the permanent teaching staff, others are subsidised but rely on voluntary assistance from dons; some are run wholly by the boys themselves without financial help.

———————

The greatest resources are commanded by Music, with five full-time teachers on the staff, and nearly forty others who give part-time instruction. Over half the boys in the school are involved in active music-making. From the top comes a regular procession of Organ Scholars, Choral Scholars, and National Youth Orchestra Players. At a more modest level there is a School Orchestra with about seventy boys in it, as well as a smaller Second Orchestra. There is a steady stream of talent into the school from the Quiristers and the Music Scholars: proficiency in music is also taken into account in the election both of academic scholars and of ordinary Commoner entrants. In terms of boy-hours per week, Music can be ranked with any of the main school subjects.

It was not always so. True the Founder insisted that scholars should be "competently instructed in plain song" as a condition of entry, so that they could play their proper part in the singing of chapel services; to assist them he made provision for three Clerks and sixteen "boy choristers" or quiristers. The College even had its own organ from the earliest days.

What happened in the next 450 years need not be recounted here: the story has already been reconstructed in loving detail by Alan Rannie in *The Story of Music at Winchester College 1394-1969*. Famous names appear on the scene from time to time. Thomas Weelkes the madrigalist, Jeremiah Clarke the composer of *The Trumpet Voluntary*, and the great Samuel Sebastian Wesley were all organists of the College. Even more important to the school was John Reading who secured a transfer from the post of Cathedral Organist in 1681 at ten times the salary and gave good value by composing the tunes for *Domum* and the Graces.

But by the mid-19th century little of the former glory, or even interest, remained. The Quiristers were given no musical training; the lay-clerks were

The earliest published edition of 'Domum' (1780). See also Appendix 2.

defective in voice as in vigour; the organists were aged or indifferent, or both. Attempts to arrange singing-classes under the Hullah system, which had been a modest success at Eton, here failed altogether; and when Fearon entered College as a little boy in 1852 his violin was taken from him on the first night of his second term by the Second Master with the warning that he "hadn't come to Winchester to idle". The Founder's desire for musical ability in his scholars had become a travesty. (see p.54). The only music-making of a serious kind was when groups of enthusiasts could persuade one of the Cathedral choir to come and teach them part-songs or anthems. For the rest there was second-rate music in Chapel to listen to, and a chance to sing a few rowdy songs on Egg-Flip night, when football victories were celebrated. Only a thirst raised by belting out a succession of popular choruses in a crowded hall could have made the foul concoction of hot beer, spices, raw eggs, brown sugar and lemon juice seem attractive. The words of these songs are preserved in old manuscript books. Some are well known favourites like *The Lincolnshire Poacher*, others have words of particular social and historical interest, like

> Right merrily sing "Live Billy our King
> For bating the tax upon Beer"

and

> Sing the soldiers cheer now the danger's past,
> The tyrant Tippoo's slain at last.

The beginning of the new era can be dated 1864 when a Glee Club was formed. The instigators were George Ridding, newly appointed Second Master, and C.H. Hawkins; the only professional musician was a Cathedral lay-clerk, Bill Hutt. The following year Hutt was made College Organist, but like a number of his predecessors in office he stayed on too long and had finally to be eased out thirty-six years later. He was also a figure easily mocked for his obesity and for the lower class accent which deprived his own name of the H and gave Wagner a "wag" like the tail of a dog. His taste, limited to Anglican Church music, was also at odds with what the school audiences, reared on jollier stuff, really wanted. So progress in musical education was halting. A Comic Vocal and Instrumental Society (1866) breathed once and expired; an attempt to form a School Choir, and do away with the Quiristers (still selected more for their "good behaviour and deserving conduct" than for any musical ability) started brightly in 1867, but within five years faded to nothing. The Glee Club concerts were popular enough, but the introduction of instrumental items was coolly received.

Things improved when in 1877 the charge of music in the school, both Glee Club and Chapel, was entrusted to Jack Toye, a well-connected and well-established housemaster, imposingly bearded and with plenty of spare weight which he was not reluctant to throw around. He was horrid to Hutt,

Bill Hutt, organist 1865-1901

who in turn took it out on the Quiristers. But he did get things moving. Glee Club increased. The choir improved. Hutt, for all his imperfections, took pupils for piano and organ. On his own initiative Hawkins secured a professional violin-teacher (one of his first pupils was E.H. Fellowes, later a concert soloist and musicologist of note), and arranged recitals of Chamber Music. Serious music started to acquire some status in the eyes of authority and of the boys. School concerts were now so well attended that College Hall was no longer big enough to house them. There was talk of building a new Concert Hall; but eighty years were to elapse before that dream materialised, and instead they took over School. During the ten years since teaching had been removed to the classrooms created by Butterfield, this fine building had lain neglected by any except wet-weather cricketers and *graffito*-carvers. Neither did its furnishings much good. Glee Club proved a better tenant, though architectural feelings had to be suppressed to tolerate the erection of an ugly stage-platform at the east end in 1882. The installation of an organ in 1886 completed the transformation.

A proper school orchestra did not come into being until 1900, although there had been a number of pioneering ventures in the ten years before. Turner's house had had enough instrumentalists to put on a series of concerts in 1891-2; and a School Band of fifes, bugles and drums was formed for the Rifle Corps in 1892. Consciousness of the need to bring these resources together in the formation of a proper orchestra was expressed in a letter to *The Wykehamist* in 1898. Jack Toye's death in 1899 (from indolence and a surfeit of cold tea, his doctors said) was a set-back. But he had musical children, and one of them, Francis, was in College at the time. With two others he assembled, so he says in his autobiography, "one double-bass, two cellos, about twenty violins and every conceivable variety of percussion". This, with an organ, made up a strange ensemble indeed. "Artistic shortcomings however are not the point at issue, which is that the orchestra, started and run without any assistance whatever from dons, immediately captured the imagination of the school. It played the kind of music they liked: it was a creation of their own. They subscribed liberally to the expenses; quite a competition started among the less musical bloods to bang the drum, clash the cymbal and tinkle the triangle. School was thronged for the concert."

This was the situation when the Governing Body finally put Bill Hutt out to grass in the Parish of Twickenham in 1901. The new Headmaster, H.M. Burge, showed his interest by securing for the school its first proper Master of Music, Dr. E.T. Sweeting. The effect was dramatic. Within two years the number of instrumentalists had risen from 28 to 80. The orchestra was put on a proper footing. A new Music School, built in the most extraordinary combination of architectural styles, was put up and fitted out at a total cost of around £11,000. Recitals were given every fortnight. A cup was presented for part-songs sung by small house choirs (1905), and additional music-teachers taken onto the staff, including Adam Carse whose simple piano arrangements are still widely used by beginners. The War put a stop to this expansion, and the school orchestra took a long time to recover. When in 1924 a cup was presented for an inter-house instrumental competition, this was more in expectation than recognition of improved standards. The first house to win it featured three soloists — an organist, a pianist, and a bagpiper.

Nothing however showed more clearly how the status of music had risen in the school than the fact that Sweeting's successor was appointed at the very top of the salary scale (nearly £1,000). George Dyson was a dapper, trim figure: with his bow-tie, stubby moustache and centre parting he looked like a senior Staff Officer. Like many small men he had enormous energy. This enabled him to combine his College work with a multitude of outside commitments — teaching, composing, lecturing, broadcasting, writing, and conducting. Not that the school suffered from this diversification. The moribund orchestra was resuscitated, and the numbers in the Glee Club rose to an all-time peak of 176. Choral and organ scholarships to Oxford and Cambridge were won for the first time. In 1936 he helped to bring about the biggest improvement of all: the Quiristers were released from their ages-old sentence of menial servitude in College Hall. With this social incubus removed they could be properly selected, properly educated

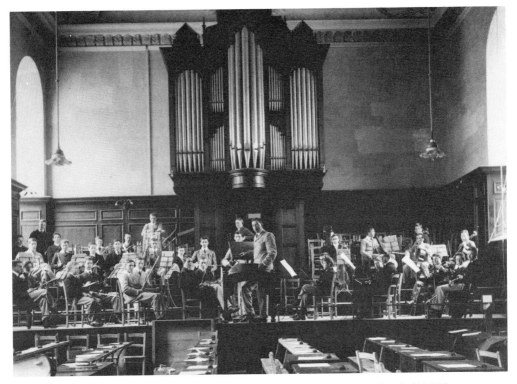

The Winchester College Orchestral Society in School (1900)

and properly trained in music. The singing in Chapel and the whole musical life of the school has been greatly enriched ever since. Quiristers are no longer the poor relations. Since the War they have regularly come into the school as Commoners, or occasionally as scholars (the first in 1948). In 1966 they were amalgamated for teaching purposes with the Pilgrims School, which also supplies the Cathedral Choir, and their record has been even better. Now it is more normal than not for Quiristers to graduate into the school, and an annual Quirister Music Scholarship provides further incentive.

One other innovation which has left a permanent mark was the founding of the Winchester Music Club. Dyson was its first conductor, and successive Masters of Music have kept up the tradition. From that time music has provided one of the strongest links between the College and the Town. The bond has been further reinforced by the institution of joint concerts in the Cathedral with other choral societies (since 1942), and by the series of Subscription Concerts which started with the building of New Hall in 1961. At most performances now there are as many local people as there are boys in the audience.

When Dyson left at the end of 1937 to be Director of the Royal College of Music (and earn himself a knighthood), he had achieved such a spread of musical activity that nearly 40% of the school took part, as players or singers, in the termly concerts. Under his successors, Sydney Watson, Henry Havergal, Christopher Cowan, Angus Watson and Keith Pusey, the general level of musicianship has continued to rise, particularly with the institution of valuable Music Scholarships: one a year since 1958, two since 1969, now seldom fewer than six. The orchestra has grown to its present size of seventy, and individuals regularly reach levels of virtuosity which enable them to tackle the great concerti: the first was David Lutyens in 1944 with the Grieg Piano Concerto, the latest include a succession of aspiring professional soloists: Robert Podolski, Adrian Adlam, Ian Fountain and Alastair Blayden, to name but a few. Sometimes as many as six players are members of the National Youth Orchestra. Even single houses of fifty to sixty boys can now produce bigger and better balanced orchestras than the entire school had under Sweeting. Former attitudes of indifference or hostility among housemasters have disappeared completely. The winning of a music competition affords as much satisfaction as beating everyone else at cricket. The musical resources of the school are so rich that they can put on a performance of the great B Minor Mass or an opera like *Carmen*, importing only the main soloists. As if that were not enough, new outlets are constantly being found: in recent times the Kingsgate Singers, the Organ Society, the Early Music Consort and Cantores Episcopi have all been expressions of a simple delight in music-making.

In musical terms this is all sheer gain, and something to be proud of. Educationally there may have been some loss as well. There is now less to attract and hold the non-musician: the gap between him and the musician grows increasingly wide. Consider Glee Club, the first organisation to popularise music in the school (I use the word "popularise" in a non-derogatory sense). At its height over a third of the boys in the school belonged to it. Not very many of them could read music, and no one with any sort of voice therefore needed to feel discouraged from joining. There was consequently a massive preponderance of Basses, very few Altos and Tenors. No matter. They would be taken through their parts note by note, and in the course of five years could be passing familiar with ten or a dozen choral masterpieces. Now the numbers in Glee Club have shrunk by a half. it is full of musicians and makes a fine noise; but fewer boys in the school have their musical education enlarged by it. And as there are fewer with choral experience, so while the Choir seldom drops below the level of excellence, the quality of congregational singing in Chapel suffers.

Again, thirty years ago attendance at a School Concert was compulsory (the most senior boys were excused in 1948). That made it necessary to retain a few popular items in the programme, like a regular Gilbert and

Quiristers serving in Hall (1922). Note the costume of Eton collar, Norfolk jacket, and knee-breeches.

Photograph: R.M. Deanesly

Sullivan number. A small enough concession. What matters is that, in the days before the packaged sound of discs and cassettes, the concerts served a noble purpose in familiarising school audiences with the classical repertoire. Further instruction came in Chapel, where the organ voluntaries often consisted of arrangements of orchestral works.

Now there is no compulsion, and very little music in the curriculum to compensate. Chapel organists take a more puristic view of their art and function. School concerts are still something of a social event, and pretty well attended: leave off the evening "toytime" provides a base but effective lure. But the rest of the concerts and recitals, put on in such rich profusion, are usually attended only by other musicians.

So in spite of all that is offered and all that is attained, there is still a fair amount of musical ignorance and tastelessness. The last actual survey of musical taste was carried out in 1949, well back in the pre-pop era, when the only choices were between "serious" and "swing". There was a 55-45 ratio favouring "serious" music: the most popular "light" composers were Arthur Sullivan and Irving Berlin. Nowadays Pop rules. Most listen to it (often perforce; even the thickest mediaeval walls cannot dampen the insistent throbbing of electronic sound); some play it. In the 1950's a Dance Band was formed, and a series of unofficial Jazz Concerts was given in Music School. Some boys even wanted to learn the guitar as a musical instrument. Authority unbent a little, and it was done. In the wake of the Beatles boys formed their own groups which were quickly relegated to the furthest building within the school's perimeter. They achieved a brief notoriety, and then passed into oblivion, only leaving behind in dusty corners a few *graffiti* in praise of "Sleepyhead" or "The Big Figure" to puzzle future generations.

The art of the painter or draughtsman is more private than that of the musician. He is not a member of a team. What he does, he does largely for his own satisfaction. The disciplines are not ones which can easily be extended to any other educational activity. Art therefore was not likely to play much of a part in schooling, at Winchester or anywhere else, so long as the interests of the individual were subordinated to the corporate claims of School or House.

There were Drawing Masters in the last century, chief among them being Richard Baigent who held the post for fifty years. He used to take a few art pupils on a private basis, but never stimulated any official interest. His best testimonial is the fine set of prints he executed in 1838 to perpetuate the memory of the Old Commoner buildings before they were demolished (see p.15).

Practice in the new Music School extension, with M. Rayson performing.
Photograph: E.A. Sollars

Ridding's decision to start Carpentry classes in 1878, following the fashion set by Thring at Uppingham, meant that a proper home for art and craft had to be found. For some years the purpose was served by renting rooms in Wolvesey, Bishop Morley's former palace. In 1891 there was even an attempt to buy the building: if successful it might have prevented the return of the Bishops of Winchester to live there in 1927. But Art was not permanently housed until 1897 when the Quingentenary Museum was built, and studio facilities were incorporated into it. By the Headmaster's personal generosity the larger gallery was also equipped with casts and portfolios of photographs for studying the history of architecture, sculpture and painting.

These installations now required the appointment of an Art Master with full teaching status. Alexander Macdonald was a person of taste and accomplishment, son of the first Principal of the Ruskin Art School in Oxford. He had a respectable degree in Classics, had learned drawing in the approved manner from a German and was reckoned a competent portraitist — qualifications which made him appear a safe enough choice in the eyes of those who associated Art in the 1890's with the diabolical forms of Oscar Wilde and Aubrey Beardsley. He was engaged at a salary of £50, which he was to supplement from the fees of individual pupils who would pay two guineas a year. However, a naturally slothful disposition, coupled with overwhelming shyness and a comfortable private income, left him disinclined to go out recruiting art pupils. It was up to the enthusiasts to seek him out for themselves. One who did was the young Kenneth Clark: he found him, he says, at his house in Kingsgate Street "sitting by the window dozing, with a volume of Pepys' diary upside down on his knee. Art was a voluntary subject and his pupils had dwindled to about three, so he seldom found the energy to visit the drawing school. He must have been dismayed by the appearance of an eager pupil."

Even the eager pupil might have been daunted by what passed for instruction: an endless routine of pencil studies made from the Museum casts. Never a glimpse of a tube of paint. Kenneth Clark persisted, comforting himself with memories of Michelangelo's apprenticeship, and won the School Drawing Prize for four years virtually unopposed. It could hardly be from this desultory treatment that the inspiration for his life's work was drawn. But there was inspiration at hand, and the source of it was Monty Rendall.

Rendall had first travelled in Europe as a student, and when he visited Italy in 1887 he was immediately intoxicated by the beauty of its countryside and its artistic past. When Fearon suggested that he should take on responsibility for founding a department of Mediaeval Art in the new Museum he fell upon the task with his usual uninhibited gusto. He spent weeks in Italy (staying with Bernard Berenson himself), in the Louvre, in the British Museum; and in the end had accumulated three hundred and twenty large photographic reproductions, elaborately mounted in walnut cabinets made to his own design. These provided the basis for his illustrated art lectures, most of them on Renaissance painters, which he started giving in 1898 and kept up until his retirement in 1924. "The art lectures" says his biographer "were mainly memorable as displays of Rendall's own personality and his exceptional power to communicate to others the glow and radiance of his own response to art. The chief significance of his enterprise lies in the fact that it was a pioneering work, a bold and successful proclamation of the value of art in education at the very time when this was most needed. For in the public schools of the nineties the arts were either unknown or suspect; if music was namby-pamby, painting was worse — half-way already to immorality. The aesthetic sense of schoolboys was therefore deliberately starved and young masters who desired the favour of their elders had to be as philistine as they could manage. Winchester was not free from the tendencies all-powerful elsewhere. Yet here was an influential member of

The east gallery of Museum, with some of the original casts still in place (1949).

Photograph: A.W. Kerr

the Staff whose virility could not be doubted, joyously waving the aesthetic banner and proving that to be virtuous it is not necessary to be a barbarian." Regular art lectures have been a feature of Winchester's cultural life ever since.

When Macdonald retired in 1922 Rendall confessed in his annual Headmaster's Report to the Governing Body: "His successor will have little to unteach: he will find hardly half a dozen pupils to teach at all". It was not entirely Macdonald's fault. Rendall had latterly been preoccupied with the War and War Memorial, and there was little support for Art among the housemasters. In Kenneth Clark's last year he had a report which suggested that he should "keep art as a hobby, and retain a sense of proportion" — which, to the delight and edification of millions, is exactly what he did.

Pondering Macdonald's failure, Rendall supposed that the boys' sensitivity to social status made them somewhat scornful of hired instructors. So he did away with the fee-system and sought the appointment of a man with impeccable credentials — one of his own favourite pupils, a Prefect of Hall, a Classical scholar with a First in Greats, a graduate of the Slade School. Dick Gleadowe was working as Secretary to the Director of the National Gallery when he allowed himself to be lured away (with a drop in salary) to serve under his former housemaster. It should have meant the realisation of Rendall's dream to "bring the whole department of visual art to a new pitch of glory" and leave a legacy of cultural refinement as his parting gift to Winchester. But Gleadowe was a Civil Servant by temperament, not a schoolmaster. His taste, draughtsmanship and sense of design were exquisite, and he has left his mark in many corners of the College buildings. The windows in College Hall, the west window in Chantry, the wrought iron gates in Meads, Frazer Tent, the bridge over Logie, the Mallory memorial in Cloisters: all these show different facets of his skill. They also brought him to public notice. The last and greatest of his commissions was the Stalingrad Sword. But for all the artistic quality of these works, they were not the sort of thing that necessarily brought teacher and pupil into closer communion. His lectures too, though more learned and wide-ranging, lacked the irresistible exuberance of Rendall's. Attendance dwindled to the "disgracefully small". He remained on the staff until his death in 1944, but his acceptance of other jobs — the Slade Professorship at Oxford, lectureships in Ireland, and a wartime post in the Admiralty — showed that Winchester was not the centre of his life. He could communicate with experts, but not so well with raw schoolboys.

Nothing represented more clearly the error of taking too refined a view of school art than the creation of a new drawing school on the top floor in Chantry. This is an exquisite room, perhaps the most beautiful in the College, with its simple vaulting and ample windows on all four sides. In

Monty Rendall, seen here with King George V on the occasion of the Royal visit of 1912.

1924 it was fitted out with oak tables and replicas of mediaeval reading desks. These furnishings complemented, even enhanced its beauty; but the narrow spiral staircase made it dauntingly inaccessible (all the furniture had to be constructed *in situ*), and it had the look of a place where even to drop a pencil-shaving would seem an offence. Brushes, palettes, rags, paint-pots, clay, plasticine, the other paraphernalia of the artist were unimaginable in that setting. It would have served nicely for a dedicated monk settling down to a few months quiet work on a manuscript, but could never have been the instrument for getting more boys interested in art.

This broadening of the appeal of art has been the work of Gleadowe's successors, Erik Sthyr and particularly Grahame Drew, with the help of a more favourable wind from the housemasters. Art still does not enjoy the status of music, but few boys will now pass through the school without some understanding of aesthetics and art history — a popular A-level course as well as a favourite div subject. Under the present Drawing Master Arthur Morgan the marvellous new Art School is well filled. Art is no longer a coterie subject, but a part of most boys' general education. It incorporates many forms of image-making, from model drawing to screen printing and sculpture. Pottery, which used to have a separate existence in the building which was until 1954 the Sanatorium laundry, has now been metamorphosed into Ceramics. There are three full time art teachers and one part time. They have little opportunity for dozing in windows or reading Pepys. Besides a full teaching timetable they have weekend tuition to give, regular excursions to London galleries and exhibitions, and a European History of Art trip to organise every Easter holidays.

Part of the liberalisation of the Victorian curriculum of Public Schools was the inclusion of handicrafts, to persuade boys that there was nothing demeaning in such work, and to equip them better for their colonial tasks. At Winchester comparatively little prominence has been given to these activities, at least until the late 1980's when C.D.T. (Craft Design Technology) started to become fashionable. For a while before 1914 carpentry actually appeared on the timetable; the place of instruction was the upper floor of the old watermill, picturesque but inadequate. By 1930 demand had risen

The upper floor of Chantry, fitted out as an Art room.

Photograph: W. Abley

The upper floor of Mill being used as a workshop (c.1920). The figure on the right is J.D. Le Couteur, an expert on stained glass.

Photograph: W. Abley

to a point where a new building was necessary, and proper workshops (still called Mill), with an extension for metalwork, were built on a scale that still seems lavish today. Now there is classwork for all in their first year, and a choice of design-based courses thereafter for those interested. The emphasis may have changed from the tradition of craftsmanship and hand skills, but Mill remains for many, dons and their wives as well as boys, an invigorating antidote to the other pressures of school life.

The Printing Society is of recent origin. Starting from nothing in 1957 when the school was unexpectedly bequeathed an ancient press and several trays of type, in time it expanded to a point where the equipment had completely outgrown its room in Museum and the passage outside. It was sheer necessity as well as professional pride that excluded visitors from the print-room, on pain of mutilation by one of the man-eating machines. Printing Society has had two lively incarnations; the first was in 1957-9 when a group of Collegemen led by Alex Reid and Philip Steadman discovered these typographic dinosaurs, taught themselves how to use them without losing their fingers, and by methods of voluntary conscription — or press-ganging — got the entire membership of the society working to produce a book of College prayers. The finished book is of fine quality, and nothing short of extraordinary considering the inexperience that lay behind it. In 1972 a dormant society was revived when Tony Ayres joined the staff. By his energy and inspiration the whole operation has been enormously enlarged: new presses, new types, new members, new standards. Much of the school's jobbing printing was done by the society, and this provided the funds for undertaking more ambitious work. In 1976, to celebrate the Caxton quingentenary, they produced an edition of Aesop's Fables, newly translated into verse, and illustrated with original wood-cuts by Richard Atkinson-Willes. That won the inter-school Printing competition, and specially bound copies were presented to the Queen and Queen Mother. In 1978 the book of prayers was reprinted; the following year the Cathedral celebrated its 900th anniversary, and the society brought out a collection of poems commissioned for the occasion, with more Atkinson-Willes woodcuts.

Printing is only one of the activities built round a society. Others have been active for well over a hundred years, and for most of them the role that they played in the early years was considerably more important, when the social, geographical, cultural, and intellectual limits were much more tightly drawn. A questing spirit restricted for much of the year to a stern regimen of Classics and rough games, and hardly ever allowed beyond the physical confines of the Cathedral Close into the town, would naturally see something very attractive in an organisation which transcended these bounds.

An interest in Natural History for instance provided a form of protection against the tedium of long afternoons spent compulsorily on Hills. The chalk yielded fossils in plenty (the name of "mouse-digger" was coined for a geologist's hammer quite early in the 19th century), and the downland was rich in flora and fauna. The formation of a Natural History Society was a happy way of channelling the interest, as well as making up for the

Below and opposite: pages from Printing Society's Aesop (1976). The text by James Sabben-Clare, the wood-cut by Richard Atkinson-Willes.

G*RAPES*
Hanging in dark clusters from the vine.
Plump
Full and juicy, ready for picking.
Leaps
To pluck them from the vine the crafty Fox.
Jumps

Falls to the ground and jumps again.
Tries
And fails. The fruit is out of reach.
Cries
"Ah let them be. I bet the grapes were sour."
So men despise what's not within their power.

deficiencies of formal Science teaching. With the whole-hearted blessing of the Headmaster, the first meeting was held in 1870 — in a classroom which also had to serve as a museum. With the opening of Moberly Library in 1871 more space was allocated to it, and the organisation took wing. There were lectures, visits, exhibitions, competitions, demonstrations. Excursions were soon being made to the New Forest and the Isle of Wight. Boys in the school read papers, often based on original research; distinguished outside speakers came to lecture on the great adventures of the 1870's — Diamond Mining at Kimberley, Deep Sea surveys, Arctic exploration, the Channel Tunnel. Almost any thing of scientific interest came within their compass, even the archaeological finds that resulted from the installation of a municipal sewage system in 1878.

After this exciting start the society dwindled and finally collapsed as Ridding's rule neared its end and he was less able to devote time to it; but its renascence in 1886 brought vigorous new growth. The entomological section was particularly strengthened by the arrival of Mottram Hewett who had an infectious love for the outdoor life, and a little-boy delight in creepy-crawlies, bird-nesting, rat-catching and fish-snaring. But the Establishment of the school regarded him and his followers with some disfavour. This is the way he begins the introduction to his little pamphlet called *Bug-hunting*: "I feel it advisable at the outset to utter a humble word or two in the hopes of propitiating those great deities, the Captains of Lords and Football, and the Senior Prefects of the various Houses . . . and the particular attribute before which I prostrate myself is the suspicion with which they regard Bughunting, considering it a dangerous pastime and liable to sap the foundations of all true manhood." I also cannot resist quoting from a slightly later book *The Open-Air Boy*, which in its gleeful emphasis on killing (rabbits with traps, sparrows with catapults, eels with spears — all for eating of course) would have caused grave offence to the modern conservationist. This is from a passage about catching rats, which have been lured to the kitchen in the night by leaving food around: "Let me advise you, unless you like the feel of a rat up your leg, to tuck your breeches into your stockings. And unless you have a dog with you, one or two rats are pretty certain to elude you, and hide till you are gone. But it is really splendid fun to be in a kitchen full of rats, with a stick and a candle. Bad for the crockery do you say? Well, perhaps! But the cook ought to have put it away. Anyway, a house cleared of rats is worth a pie-dish or two."

Hewett was in charge of the Natural Science section when the new Museum was built. The Society now had more space, for meetings, books, and display-cabinets which were soon filled with collections of specimens. Apart from one other brief period of dormancy at the beginning of the century, dispelled by the institution of Natural History prizes in 1904, it has continued a vigorous existence ever since. Only its character has changed somewhat over the years. Once it was carefully structured and beset by rules, with membership only by election and attendance by invitation. That has all gone: now it is mainly patronised by younger boys, as only the most dedicated of the senior ones manage to find time for it. It has always provided its own kind of humour, often unintentional: early lectures included "The Homing Pigeon" by A. Sparrow, and a College-man talking, from personal experience some would say, on "some Low Forms of Life"; a report on a demonstration by a taxidermist concluded triumphantly "In less than an hour he had stuffed an unprepared starling." But it also serves a more serious purpose. First findings of several new hybrid orchids can be credited to the society (one, *Gymnaplatanthera Jacksonii* even bears the name of its discoverer, H. A. Jackson); and significant contributions have been made to national surveys of flora and fauna — in 1962 it published its own booklet on the birds of the Winchester District. A number of professional naturalists owe their initiation to the activities of the Nat. Hist. Soc.; but for most of its members its attraction is that it provides a chance to get out of Winchester, to immerse themselves in a world quite different from their routine work, to experience the keen pleasure of hearing the nightingales in Crab Wood, trapping Hawk Moths in the water meadows, collecting fungi in the New Forest, and finding fossilised sharks' teeth in the caenozoic clay-beds of Lee-on-Solent.

The N.H.S. begat two offspring which had originally been part of it. The Photographic Society began life in 1894 under the care of L.L. Garbutt, and expertly helped by Walter Abley who was a laboratory technician for fifty years. Many of Abley's glass-plate negatives still survive, preserving forgotten scenes in miraculous detail. Monty Rendall too was an indefatigable photographer and has left a full pictorial record of school life in the first quarter of the century. With the help of recent members of Phot. Soc. several of these old photographs are incorporated into this book.

The Archaeological section parted company from the parent stock in 1895, and rapidly came to provide one of the richest forms of extramural activity. Not only does the Winchester area itself, with a continuous history of human occupation going back to the Iron Age, furnish inexhaustible material for the study of the past; but the energy of successive presidents and the lure of places beyond the College bounds have carried members of Arch. Soc. ever further afield in search of the jewels of European culture — on foot to St. Cross, by bicycle to Romsey, car to Salisbury (Rendall used to organise an annual walk/run to Stonehenge), bus to Bath, train to London, ferry to Normandy, aeroplane to Athens. But the society is not just a tourist organisation: on top of lectures and visits, its members have regularly undertaken their own field-work and research. A particularly active period between the wars produced two books, on Winchester City and College, which are still authoritative sources, and a "dig" on St.

Catherine's Hill which revealed both mediaeval and Iron Age remains. The leaders of these enterprises, Nowell Myres and Christopher Hawkes, carried their youthful interest forward into later life with great distinction. And they are but two from a notable list of Wykehamist archaeologists. Many are still active today, including no less than six who were at school in the 1960's: one became Professor of Egyptology in Oxford before he was 30, another Director of the British School in Iraq at a similar age, another came to supervise the excavation of a large Romano-British cemetery in Winchester just a few years after he had first worked on it as a boy in the school. The publication of *Winchester Studies III* with a record of this Lankhills dig is the latest testimonial to the abiding Wykehamist interest in archaeology.

The oldest of all the school societies was founded in 1862. C.H. Hawkins, the moving spirit of so many innovations, found when he came to the staff that the cultural life of the school was a barren desert. Studying the classical texts week after week with an eye only for grammatical detail, the boys had no idea what literature was. So he founded a Shakespeare Society. Observing the protocol of the time, he limited its members at first to the twelve senior boys in the school: they met on winter evenings at his house in College Street, and read plays and talked about them in an atmosphere far removed from the frigid formality of most of the dealings between boys and masters. From these readings there naturally developed a desire to present the plays in full dramatic dress. There had been theatricals of a kind before — R.B. Mansfield's book describes a performance held in Seventh Chamber in the 1830's on a stage made of bed-boards, paper, and string — but nothing above the level of pantomime. This was altogether different. In a series of productions between 1865 and 1868 the hall of New Commoners was adapted for performances of Shakespeare's major tragedies. Most of the rehearsing was done in the holidays and the plays were performed at the very beginning of term. The leading roles were all played by Hawkins himself — without the enormous beard which later covered half his face. In the manner of the times, and as a palliative to restless schoolboy audiences, the tragedies were given comic postludes; sharing the bill with Hamlet was "Little Toddlekins" with King Lear was "The Irish Tutor: twenty minutes with a tiger."

Once Hawkins took over his boarding house (1869), and Commoner Hall was converted into classrooms, the performances stopped. But the Shakespeare Society carried on: with new members and the addition of a musical element it became the Shakespeare Reading and Orpheus Glee United Society, or SROGUS for short. Ladies were admitted as audience, and on occasions were even allowed to take part — one of the first breaches of the monastic wall. On a memorable summer afternoon in 1896 Hawkins had a marquee erected on his lawn for a reading of Antony and Cleopatra

C.H. Hawkins as Hamlet (1866), and a scene from Little Toddlekins.

which was to star a professional actress ("she used to act with Irving at the Lyceum" the boys said).

In 1900 the presidency was taken over by Monty Rendall, and for a quarter of a century it became an institution highly coloured by his own distinctive personality. He read all the main parts himself, heedless of the incongruity of squeezing his ungainly figure into the delicate mould of a Hamlet or a Romeo. Around him he collected a circle of the cleverest and most handsome boys in the school, mostly from College. In the dignified setting of the Second Master's or Headmaster's house, before an invited audience, the readings took on an importance rather beyond their literary value. They provided a taste of a politer world, a peculiarly English mode of civilization where art and emotion were decorously clad in evening dress and the obscurities of Elizabethan diction.

Of all the school societies, SROGUS was the last to abandon its dinner-jacketed traditions. It survived in its old form until about 1960, underwent transformation into a less hieratic Drama Society, popped up again once or twice for special occasions, and then disappeared. What finally undermined it was not its social exclusiveness, but the fact that it was no longer wanted. Plays were now being read in the divs and in the House and had no need of a mystic circle; more important, live drama was playing an increasing part in the life of the school.

The productions in Commoner Hall in the 1860's had no follow up. Part of the reason was the lack of facilities: there was no hall available until School was vacated, and even when a stage platform was installed there, the producer still had the encumbrance of a large organ to get round. Behind scenes there was no spare room at all, only a dark and dusty hole under the stage where waiting actors had to crouch in tense discomfort. Not until after the first War did any sort of theatrical tradition establish itself. College mounted a series of classic productions in Hall (Shakespeare, Sheridan, Marlowe, Yeats), and Cyril Robinson presented a number of ancient dramas in his own House. Plays in French and Greek were performed by members of those departments. Fresh impetus was provided by the arrival on the staff of Ronald Hamilton who brought an eye for detail, a panache, a love for everything theatrical, born of fruitful days with the Cambridge A.D.C. His first production, *Les Fourberies de Scapin*, was in 1934; his last, a musical version of *The Comedy of Errors*, in 1969. Between the two he put on about fifteen others, ranging from light revue to the mighty Passion Play which was acted in the Cathedral on occasions when the school had not gone home before Easter. But the culmination of all his achievements was the production of the Masque written in 1961 to celebrate the opening of New Hall. For a full week it played to packed houses and delighted thousands with its musical and verbal wit, its liveliness, its style, its pageantry. Notices glowed from the pens of amateur and professional critics up and down the country. *The Times* was particularly fulsome. A reporter in *Die Zeit*, after watching a day of cricket and an evening of the Masque, thought he had come close to understanding at least one facet of the English character. As for the show, "was it the sort which induces quiet sleep even before the rise of the curtain, while reading the programme? Not at all. It was a production of such perfection that London papers wrote that it must be performed as soon as possible in the capital (That, of course, was almost an insult. Members of the school and masters here regard a success in Winchester as more important than one in London)."

The building of New Hall with its spacious auditorium, wide stage, and well appointed Green Rooms encouraged the regular performance of school plays for the first time in nearly a hundred years. However it was not a setting to attract the less ambitious or experienced producer: erecting the proscenium was laborious, the vocal acoustic was demanding, and there were not enough resources for lighting so large a stage area. There was also some awkwardness over the fact that productions with girls in them had not been envisaged when the building was designed: there was only one dressing-room.

Opposite: Ronald Hamilton taking a cameo part in his own production of 'Le Bourgeois Gentilhomme' (1967).   *Photograph: E.A. Sollars*

The real change came from two not unrelated events: first the advent in 1968 of a Headmaster with personal experience of directing school plays and a belief in the educational value of drama; second the conversion of the old gymnasium into a small theatre. For a dozen years it was a Theatre Workshop, little but a wooden floor, bare brick walls patterned in the Victorian high Gothic style, seats of excruciating discomfort, and simple but adequate staging facilities. In 1982 it was imaginatively improved by the Ted Cullinan partnership, and, graced by a royal audience in May of that year, celebrated its upgrading by taking on the name of the Queen Elizabeth II Theatre. In the eighteen years since the first conversion, far more plays have been put on in the school than in the previous hundred. New Hall is now used comparatively little for drama — which is just as well in view of the ever increasing number of concerts it houses; but it remains still a perfect setting for the really spectacular productions like the two Purcell operas of 1976 and 1979, *The Magic Flute* (1981), *Fidelio* (1982) and *Carmen* (1988).

From Act I of the Masque which celebrated the opening of New Hall (1961): the Fellows swear never to wear red shoes.

Photograph: E.A. Sollars

From Act III of the Masque (1961): S. Woodward as the footballer who is 'not non-plussed by a lovely bust'.

Photograph: E.A. Sollars

There are now eight to ten plays put on most years. It may be that there is still not quite as much drama done as in some other schools. There is no Head of Drama on the staff; there are no acting competitions; productions tend to happen when the spirit moves, and most houses have only done a handful of plays in the whole span of their existence. Nevertheless drama is, second only to music, the most widely practised, enjoyed and respected artistic activity in the school today. By contrast most of the other pursuits described in the last few pages now have a less important role to play than they used to. Most of them were started in an attempt to extend the narrow boundaries of school life and curriculum. Nowadays there is not the same need, with so many different subjects on the timetable, and such a multitude of opportunities to go out and see things for oneself. There is less attraction in a classroom lecture on dinosaurs, early steam-engines, Rembrandt or Wren churches, when a boy can catch a train to London after lunch, spend the afternoon making his own discoveries in museums and art galleries, and be back in time for tea. Another reason for the decline of the old school societies is the increased pressure, chiefly from examinations, upon senior boys. Until about 1960 when A-levels started to be taken seriously it was expected that most of the lectures at society meetings would be given by members who had "mugged up" a subject themselves. It was a valuable method of self-education. This is simply no longer possible.

Historically the societies played an important part in enlightening the Wykehamist, to the point where natural history was no longer regarded as likely to sap the foundations of manhood, nor art as the refuge of those who could not play games. They still have a contribution to make. The most recent development is the growth of more intellectual societies where lectures on matters of scientific, literary, historical and philosophical interest regularly command large audiences. In the proceedings of the societies called after them the names of Arnold Toynbee and William Empson are brought to the attention of another generation of Wykehamists.

Chapter VIII

Tradition and Ceremony

The Public Schools of the last century were in many respects tribal societies: they were self-contained and largely self-governing, with a complex set of regulations and conventions whose enforcement was necessary to mark the gradations of power in the hierarchy. Every little advance in seniority earned an extra privilege, jealously guarded, however petty, as a means of separating a boy from those below him in status. And so that even the humblest junior should be invited to feel that membership of this society was itself a privilege, initiation ceremonies were invented to test his capacity to set foot on the ladder.

A former housemaster who was at Winchester in the 1850's described such an ordeal thus: "On arrival in Commoners, new men were herded into Good Friday Passage, told to climb over the door, along the top and over into Grass Court on the other side. While they did this, 'swell men' shied at them with india-rubber balls. But they refrained from shying at me because I looked nicer than the rest." Much greater cruelty is evidenced from earlier days: "When I was a boy at Winchester, it was the custom to give each newcomer what was called 'tin gloves'. The unfortunate scholar had his hands held by a prefect and on the backs of them a cross was burnt in with a 'hot end' or piece of burning stick. This was supposed to give him the power of handling hot articles without flinching — a faculty which, in his capacity of fag, cook, toaster, and stoker, would no doubt have been highly valuable . . . I carry my cross to this day, and, in common with most of the Wykehamists of my time, shall carry it to my grave."

Such instances of savagery belong only to a short and undisciplined period of Winchester's history, and can be matched in brutality by the customs of any other school of the time. Even today a new boy, whatever his school, is liable to be exposed to some sort of humiliation before he is allowed to "belong". At Winchester there are still some vestiges of the milder practical jokery to which the 19th century novitiate had to submit — for instance the *Pempe*. What happens in College is this. After about ten days of his first term a new boy is asked (rhetorically) by the *pater* who is responsible for his well-being, whether he has got his *Pempe*. No? Well he had better go and ask the Senior Inferior for it. Who is the Senior Inferior? That he must find out. He does so, and dutifully asks him for a *Pempe*. No luck: perhaps the College Organist can help. He too is traced, but proves no more obliging. Can the Captain of Basketball give him a *Pempe*? He can't, and so the chase goes on until someone finally takes pity and provides him with what he wants. It is a slip of paper on which is written (if he gets his Greek right) the words *pempe pempe ton moron protero*, that is, "send send the fool further".

This simple game, now at least 150 years old, is in fact a harmless way of teaching the identity and function of other boys in the house. Another picturesque ceremony, which had more of the features of an initiation, lasted until 1954. It is best described in the words of a little boy writing home to his sisters in 1891: "Last Thursday all the new boys, myself amongst them, had to go up Hills with our 'paters' that is boys told off to teach us our notions. When we got half way up we had to run down 'chalk-pit' and up again. When we got to the top, we had to walk out of 'Clump' blindfold — Clump is the clump of trees on the top — then we had to run through a 'maze', a labyrinth up there. Then we had to see 'Domum Cross' and kiss a knuckle-bone on it. I do not know if, when Mother and Father went up there, they looked over the other side; if they did they saw a tremendously steep grassy slope, beyond which stands up another very steep high down called 'Twyford Down'. Down the first slope you had to run and up the next one, a distance of about half a mile. After this we had to walk over the river on a plank turned edgeways about 4 in. wide, no easy matter I can tell you. Then we went back and had to throw a stone over a building called 'Mill'. All this I accomplished successfully, and now I shall not be a full blown Wykehamist till I have been tunded (beaten) twice."

Acceptance into the Wykehamist tribe still marked only the beginning of a long period of assimilation. For in the course of five centuries Winchester had accumulated more peculiarities of custom and speech than any other school; in fact the special significance of the term "notion" first applied to these usages around 1860, has become widely enough known to land a place in the Concise Oxford Dictionary.

The "notions" which a boy would have to learn consisted of the vocabulary peculiar to Winchester, special names for people and places, and the things that one must and must not do. The volume of information was such that boys took to compiling their own glossaries, and many are still preserved. The earliest of them, dated c.1840, contains about 350 words; by the end of the century the number had risen to a thousand, though

College Officers taking tea in Chamber Court (1861). Note the 'cowshooter' hats. Of the two figures in the centre, the one on the left is Herbert Stewart, later a Major-General, who lost his life heroically in the Sudan, and on the right Trant Bramston.

many were by that time obsolete. Most of the word-books were compiled with a care born of devotion and long leisured hours, with illuminated capitals and exquisite pen-drawings; others are illustrated with contemporary photographs and documents. In themselves they form a fascinating record of the Victorian age at Winchester; but there is as much interest in the words themselves. Students of philology started to examine them about a hundred years ago. The first to produce a full etymological commentary on the Winchester notions was R.G.K. Wrench, a small and irascible German teacher nicknamed "Piggy". Much of the work in his *Winchester Word Book* of 1891 still stands, though a good deal was added to it, particularly comparisons with regional dialects, by the Three Beetleites, whose *Winchester College Notions* has long remained the standard authority. Now that too has been superseded by the compilation of Charles Stevens, the result of more than fifty years' examination of the available sources and much scholarly insight; to his manuscripts I am greatly indebted for much of what follows.

The notions books contain hundreds of quaint and curious names for places, people, and objects. There was Gundry's Hole, and Gunner's Hole, and Pulver's Dust Hole; there was Jemima and Joel and Juppiter on Olympus; there were jeroboams and benjamins and nebuchadnezzars. Behind each of these names there was a history or an explanation: Gunner was the name of a College Chaplain who donated a stretch of the river Itchen for use as the school bathing-place; Joel was the Under Porter, being only a minor prophet; and benjamin was a ruler, as Psalm 68 verse 27 will tell you.

Such coinages have their parallels in other schools. It may be that there are more of them at Winchester because there is a bigger tradition to build on, and because it was for generations a regular form of amusement to invent and propagate new notions in the hope that they would catch on. However what gives the Winchester vocabulary its particular interest is the survival of word-forms from earlier periods, centuries after they have dropped out of ordinary speech. There are still in use, or were until very recently, quite a number of words which are pure Anglo-Saxon (modern meanings are given in brackets): to *mug* (study), *thoke* (leisure, time off), a *brock* (misfortune), *cud* (smart, nice). Other direct links with the distant past are Latin words: *licet* (permissible), *preces* (prayers), *remedy* (holiday — a meaning given to *remedium* in mediaeval times), *continent* (confined to bed), *foricas* (lavatory).

In the 19th century the stock of notions was greatly increased. Common Victorian slang supplied words like *dibs* (money): the Winchester tariff of exchange from sixpence to sovereign was 2 *tizzies* for a *shig*, 5 *shigs* for a *bull*, 4 *bulls* for a *sog*. From local Hampshire dialect came *scob* (a desk), *spree* (conceited), *pitch-up* (friends or relations), and many others; from further afield came *brum* (penniless) based on the Kentish *brumpt* (bankrupt), *teejay* (Commoner equivalent of *pater*) from the French *protégé*, and *bangy* (brown

Title-page from the Commoner Word Book of H.E. Campbell (1868).

sugar), an abbreviation of Bangalore which exported it. A special instance
of the way meanings were transferred is provided by the word *quill* which
at Winchester means anything that takes one's fancy; as a verb, or in the
phrase "to raise a quill" it means to win favour or ingratiate. The first
dictionary meaning of *quill* is a narrow, hollow stem, such as that which
runs up the middle of a feather; but in Devonian dialect it had particular
significance as a faucet for a cask, so to tap liquor by this means, hence

to ply Parliamentary electors with drink, and so to the Wykehamical sense of currying favour. An extraordinary journey of association.

But by no means all Winchester speech is of this exotic kind. There are familiar words too which have been subjected to inglorious metamorphosis. The ending *-er* or *-ers* was picked up from common speech and widely applied so that exercise became *ekker*, Cathedral *Cathers*, names-calling *namers* and so on. By an even greater barbarism words were shorn of their endings altogether, leaving long final vowels vulgarly exposed. The contraction of words like "examination" and "competition" into *examina* and *competi* is sanctioned by the practice of ancient scribes; but Winchester makes a speciality of coinages like *gymna*, *steeplecha*, and *mathma*, and where whimsy and euphony take a hand can even convert so mundane an object as the Dons Common Room Notice Board into the outlandish Do.Co.Ro.No.Bo.

The deliberate creation of notions in the past was largely a pastime of scholars, and exemplifies just those qualities of mind — a fondness for learned allusion, *double entendre*, and linguistic agility — which are nowadays the mark of the crossword champion. A few examples, some amusing, most of them obscure or simply excruciating will show what I mean. Prefects with half-power were called *Bluchers*, because the Marshal of that name used to wear half-boots; a bowler hat was called a *cowshooter* because it was a distant relation of the deerstalker; a tea-caddy was called *tudoces* because the Latin *tu doces* means "thou teachest": the Porter's Lodge was referred to as *Skiers*, because when abbreviated in standard Wykehamical fashion to Po.Lo. it formed the Latin word *polo* which means "in the sky". I think that will be enough. Maybe it is consoling to reflect that the more far-fetched the etymology, the shorter the life-expectancy of a notion was. All of these extraordinary examples have long since passed out of use.

Even so there was a great deal for the new boy to learn, and his initial bewilderment is succinctly and wittily expressed in these lines from the 1961 Masque written by Michael Burchnall. They are sung by four very small boys:

We're baffled by these awful monosyllables — like Firk
And Spree and Tug and Brew and Mug and Brum and Thick
   and Shirk,
And Cad and Cud and Hot and Jig and Sweat and Toys and Slabs;
If this is what we're in for — then we might as well Toll Abs,
   Though we haven't got a notion what it means.
How *can* we tell that Armoury is *not* called Gunner's Hole?
That Baker doesn't mean a man who's Bringing Down a Roll?
You show a don your fountain pen, and he says 'What a quill!'
There are no pegs for Hunter Tent, no miller grinds in Mill . . .
   O, we haven't got a notion what it means.

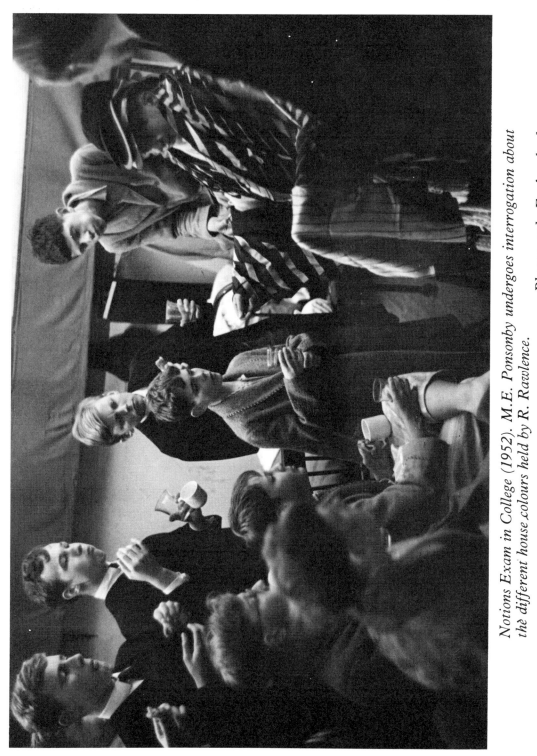

Notions Exam in College (1952). M.E. Ponsonby undergoes interrogation about the different house colours held by R. Rawlence.

Photograph: E. Auerbach

After a fortnight of term the new boy underwent a Notions Exam. This had once been a serious ordeal with dire punishments for ignorance visited upon both the junior and his mentor. However the Great Tunding Row of 1872, when the flogging of a senior Commoner for not knowing his notions caused weeks of public outrage, (see p.44) reduced it to a more homely affair. The seriousness with which it is now taken varies very much from house to house. In College it has long been an opportunity for chamber feasting and a parade of those notions where question and answer have achieved the status of ritual formulae, a meaningless rigmarole typified by this sort of exchange: Q. "Which way does College clock face?" A. "Into Mrs. Bendle's boudoir". The College clock has no face, nor, I doubt, did the wife of the odd-job man ever boast a boudoir.

A great deal of this arcane language has been pared away as recent generations of pupils have reacted against the exclusiveness of the society they lived in, or as the call for such colourful profusion of vocabulary has diminished in the mish-mash of mid-Atlantic mid-cultural speech. The only words whose passing is really to be regretted are those which genuinely enrich the language. The editor of *The Trusty Servant* wrote in 1957: "'Tug' and 'Brock' and 'Quill' will presumably never go; as it is, it is hard to see how the ordinary Englishman gets on without them." But dying they are, some after a full thousand years of active service, and will soon be fit matter only for the antiquarian.

There is less cause to mourn the passing of many of the notions of behaviour — the conventions based on petty privilege, which determined what a boy should or should not do. A forthright new boy wrote home in 1896: "Everything here is so different, they have such extraordinary ideas about things, one thing is that you have your coat buttoned up all your first half (half is the word for term) and you are allowed to unbutton one button every half you have been here, also you have to wear a top hat all Sunday, it is awful rot, you can imagine that I look a toff in a top hat." There were many other such notions, a few perpetuating mediaeval traditions like the practice of saluting as you walked under Middle Gate because the statue of the Blessed Virgin Mary was lodged there, but mostly the invention of status-conscious Victorian schoolboys. The exigencies of the Second World War did away with much of this nonsense, the Prefect of Hall enunciating the principle that "notions preventing people on account of youth from doing things that are convenient and good for them, or against which there are no reasons, should be allowed to die." Since then, as the barriers between age-groups have been yet further reduced, so the need to preserve the outward forms of distinctiveness has dissolved as well.

By comparison with the school of 1900, or even 1950, the number of peculiarities of speech and comportment still being observed is really quite small. But it would be wrong to suppose that a sort of cultural revolution

Top hats for Sunday. (Left) R.O. Hall and C.A.S.S. Gordon (1932), (Right) E.P. Moon and G.F. Higginson (1922).
Photograph: R.M. Deanesly

had swept away all links with the traditional past. Institutions that are quaint, even absurd, survive for no better reason than that they have long done so, and there has been no pressing need to change. To disbelieving parents of first-year boys the Headmaster admits in an annual speech that the school only meets regularly as a unified body twice a year — and that is on top of St. Catherine's Hill at eight o'clock in the morning at the beginning of the summer and winter terms. This ceremony of "Morning Hills" was invented by one of the great traditionalists, W.A. Fearon, in 1894 as a vestigial reminder of the days when the organised processions to Hills provided boys with their only opportunity for outdoor recreation. The processions were discontinued in 1868 when mass absenteeism had made them an embarrassment to authority. Fearon's other purpose was to maintain the Wykehamist's right to disport himself on Hills as he had done for three centuries or more. This right was of a somewhat tenuous nature as the land belonged to the Church, and it took some heavy string-pulling to discourage the lessee from fencing it off in 1878. Only when the Old Wykehamist masonic Lodge purchased the land in 1930 and handed it over to the school did the right become absolute.

The Morning Hills ceremony consists simply of an assembly, with a prayer or two, and then a names-calling of the whole school. For a senior boy or for any of the dons who have bestirred themselves to attend, it is all over in five minutes, barely a tenth of the time it takes to walk there and back. But the experience of seeing the early morning mists rising off the Itchen valley below is one of unforgettable beauty, and amply repays the unwonted expenditure of effort at such an hour.

Fearon also tried to revive the old custom of "going *circum*". The trouble here was that though the phrase cropped up in some of the early documents, no one knew exactly what it meant. The most likely explanation is that until Reformation times there was a daily procession round the Cloisters of the kind prescribed in the New College statutes; and that even after this practice had ceased the name continued to be applied to the saying of private prayers in the ambulatory between Chapel and Cloisters. There was also a quite separate institution on the last morning of the summer term when the scholars processed round Chamber Court singing the morning hymn *Iam lucis orto sidere* before dispersing (Bishop Ken's translation "Now that the daylight fills the sky" is No.1 in *Hymns Ancient and Modern*). That was discontinued in 1863 when George Ridding, who described himself as being "not of a processional mind" became Second Master.

Fearon brought the two ceremonies together and for the ten years 1887-97 made it part of a morning service held towards the end of March in honour of the Founder to have the whole school processing round Cloisters singing *Iam lucis*.

Though this has been long since forgotten, the ends of the term and the year are still celebrated in traditional ways. On the last night of the winter term there is *Illumina*. As the December evening darkens, stubs of candles are lit in the little niches called *Temples* which abound in the mediaeval walls around Meads, and a large bonfire blazes on the edge of the ball court behind School. The effect is sometimes enlivened by the surreptitious insertion of fireworks and other explosive devices into the flames; but even without the bangs the sight of all the pinpricks of light suspended in the gloom is entrancing.

The custom seems to be of quite recent origin by Winchester standards. Until 1862 Meads was divided by a wall separating the Commoners' small Grass Court from the rest of the field, which was the exclusive preserve of the scholars. At the end of the winter term before this barrier was to be removed, the Commoners decided to celebrate the event by putting lighted candles in the old bit of wall bounding the west side of Grass Court. No doubt many niches existed already where the mortar had decayed and the flints had fallen out: others were made for the occasion. For the next few years, until the Commoners were all distributed to boarding houses in 1869, they kept up the annual commemoration. Then the custom was taken over by College: it was after all a convenient and picturesque way of using up the candle-stubs that had accumulated over the year (candles provided bedside lighting in the upstairs chambers of College until 1934); nowadays they have to be bought for the occasion.

Until the early 1960's, when it became usual for boys to leave in

(Above) Morning Hills with A.T.P. Williams presiding, and J.E. Pretty, Prefect of Hall, calling names (1931).
(Below) The last boys to be moved out of 'New Commoners' and into boarding houses (1869).

December straight after winning places at Oxford or Cambridge, the normal leaving time was July. Hence the end of the summer term was an occasion for heightened merry-making tinged with nostalgia, and even in the truncated form of festivities observed today there are many traces left of a more elaborate ceremonial.

The last week of the term used to be Election week, when scholars were elected both to the Winchester and to the Oxford foundations. The examiners coming from Oxford were welcomed at the gates with the *Oratio Ad Portas* which had been instituted in 1615 by Mrs. Letitia Williams, a lady of strong Wykehamical connections and Royalist sympathies: the speaker received 13s 4d. for his pains. This practice stopped in 1873, a few years after competition for the New College scholarships had ceased to be restricted to Wykehamists. But the *Ad Portas* speeches have been preserved in a different form. Since 1883 they have been used as instruments of welcome to people of distinction — chiefly Wykehamists, but Royalty, Prime Ministers and others as well. The school forms a hollow square in Chamber Court. The Prefect of Hall delivers a laudatory address in Latin, and the visitor replies in whatever terms he feels to be appropriate (for much of this century Latin was considered as *de rigueur* for the recipient as well, but there is now a reversion to English). Recent honorands have been Lord Clark, Sir Arnold Toynbee (who at the age of 85 showed an astonishing ability to *ad lib* in Latin), the Bishop of Winchester, Lord Carver, Kingman Brewster, nine Old Wykehamists judges, Lord Whitelaw, and Her Majesty the Queen.

Election week was also marked by a series of grand dinners. These have been replaced by a single "Domum" dinner on the last night of term. The Domum, that is, "homewards" celebrations begin a little earlier in the afternoon with "Medal Speaking". Winchester has no Prize Day of the usual kind when parents swelter in uncomfortable finery, applaud politely the winner of the Junior Handicrafts Prize, and nod discreetly through the uplifting orations of the Headmaster and the Distinguished Guest Speaker. Medal Speaking by contrast is a very esoteric, low-key affair. The first medals were presented in 1761, and every year until 1792, by Lord Bruce, later Earl of Ailesbury: they were awarded for composition and declamation (in Latin and English), and on a day chosen to coincide with the Winchester Races, so that "a very brilliant company" would be assembled, the winners gave a public performance of their pieces. After a brief gap, coinciding with a period of rebelliousness, medals were again given annually from 1797 onwards by the Prince of Wales. When he succeeded to the throne as King George IV in 1820 the medals, two gold and two silver, became a royal gift, and have remained so ever since. From the mid-19th century Medal Speaking has been part of the Domum celebrations and the form has remained unchanged. Before an audience of dons in their academic robes, and a small number of other guests, all the major prize-winners in addition to the

The Prime Minister, Stanley Baldwin, being received Ad Portas in 1928.
Photograph: H.W. Salmon

medallists come forward in turn. If they have a speech or recitation to perform, they do so; then they are presented to the Warden or Headmaster who makes a few complimentary remarks; a handshake or presentation; decorous applause, and so to the next man. It is a simple, dignified, and pleasing ceremony — and not overlong.

Domum Dinner follows. This used to be rather a tedious affair, attended by the Fellows, the dons and the whole of College, with an endless series of speeches — at least ten in 1876 for instance — keeping impatient little boys rooted to their hard benches. A further blight was the inclusion on the menu of a traditional dish called Stuckling, made of new green apples, minced meat, and caraway, cooked in a hard pastry case; by all accounts it was quite uneatable. In time senior Commoners came to replace the College juniors, and nowadays the occasion is made into a dinner for all the year's leavers, with the number of speeches drastically reduced, and no Stuckling.

The most traditional part of Domum Day is the conclusion, when members of the Winchester community mingle in the Warden's Garden as dusk settles and the Band plays. There used also to be a Domum Ball, but it was discontinued in 1904 when it ceased to be profitable. The song from which the name Domum is taken was composed in the 17th century.

Domum being celebrated in Meads on the occasion of the Quingentenary (1893).

The Queen presenting her silver medal for English Speech to C.T. Godfrey-Faussett at the Sixth Centenary Ad Portas (1982)

Photograph: Bill Warhurst, The Times.

There is a long-standing legend that the words of *Dulce domum* were written by a boy who was detained in Winchester during the holidays, and obligingly carved them on a tree by the river before pining away. The story is too absurd to contemplate. For the most plausible account I draw again upon Charles Stevens' researches: he makes out a strong case for supposing that the lyrics were the work of a group of boys lodged at a farm in Crawley, a few miles out of Winchester, when the Plague of 1666 had closed down the school at around Whitsun. The tune to which they are now sung clearly does not fit them at all, and presumably the College organist John Reading who composed it a few years later had little idea of the working of Latin metre. *Dulce domum* had been adopted as the school song by at least the mid-18th century, and used to be sung repeatedly at different places around the school grounds during the last weeks of the school year. Nowadays it is reserved for School Concerts and Domum Day itself. The tune is awkward, too wide in range for many adolescent voices, but the words avoid the mawkishness of many school songs and the chorus ends with a satisfying shout.

The setting, the company, the associations of Domum make it an emotional occasion. But in a hard-headed world there is still room for indulging a bit of sentiment. The traditions of Winchester remain an important part of the fabric of its life, but they are not allowed to ossify or to obstruct the continued pursuit of ideals. The prevailing attitude may be stated in the words of George Ridding, who certainly had no great respect for tradition himself. In a sermon preached in 1873 he said: "Veneration for the past ennobles if it kindles enthusiasm and stirs emulation; it degrades if it checks ideas and limits aspiration. If customs which never would be introduced into any new school, were made perpetual in an old one, because it was the tradition, and no real son of the school would think of altering such an old custom; if refinements of life and methods of study, which would be adopted in a new school, should be rejected as unheard of in an old one; if standards of feeling, language or morality in school life, which would be condemned as below the spirit of the times, were maintained in an old school . . . then in such ways the inheritance of antiquity would mar its ennobling associations by a very real degree of degradation . . . The axe is set to the root of the tree."

The school in procession down College Street for the Quingentenary Service in the Cathedral (1893). See p.79.

Medal Speaking 1981. Murray Botes, winner of the Queen's Gold Medal for English Essay faces John Thorn (Headmaster) and Lord Aldington (Warden).

EFFICIEM SERVI SI VIS SPECTARE PROBATI
QUISQVIS ES HÆC OCULOS PASCAT IMAGO TUOS
PORCINUM OS QUOCUN QUE CIBO JEJUNIA SEDAT
HÆCSERA CONSILIUM NE FLUAT ARCTA PREMIT
DAT PATIENTEM ASINUS DOMINIS JURGANTIBUS AUREN
CERVUS HABET CELERES IRE REDIRE PEDES
LÆVA DOCET MULTUM TOT REBUS ONUSTA LABOREM
VESTIS MUNDITIEM DEXTERA APERTA FIDEM
ACCINCTUS CLADIO CLYPEO MUNITUS & INDE
VEL SE VEL DOMINUM QUO TUEATUR HABET

A young scholar points out the virtues of the Trusty Servant to a meek-looking Quirister (from the Graphic, 1872). Compare the Quirister's uniform with that shown on p.123.

Chapter IX

Service to the Community

If you had asked a Wykehamist at any time before unemployment became a serious problem what he thought the long-term purpose of his education was, he might well have talked in terms of "service to the community". This at any rate would have been the likely response of his teachers; just after the Second War a boy who had left a little before and was now contemplating an artistic career was told by his erstwhile housemaster that this was "irresponsible and unWykehamical".

Within the school concern for others was supposedly developed by the prefectorial system whereby senior boys governed the conduct of younger ones, and this was a notion not just dating from Arnold of Rugby (himself a Wykehamist and a friend of George Moberly) with whom it is traditionally associated, but as old as the foundation itself. In Rubric XXXIV of his Statutes for the College Wykeham determined that in each Chamber there should be three older boys who would supervise the studies of their fellows, and report on their moral and intellectual progress to the authorities. Such an overseeing role could of course be educative for both parties, but it was also open to abuse as during the 19th century the power wielded by prefects increased towards absolutism and included the right of chastisement. Practice in coercion and self-indulgence could not be much of a preparation for life. Nowadays when most of the task of maintaining discipline has reverted to the housemaster, the duties of prefects are much more closely related to what Wykeham originally intended. But the diminution of their powers correspondingly reduces the amount they can learn about responsibility. It is obvious that the school system by itself cannot complete this function of their education; it is also necessary to have some idea of what happens in the world outside, to know a little about the needs of those whom one is intending to serve. However to combine such understanding with the restricted life and activities of school is a very difficult thing, as all Headmasters have appreciated. Spencer Leeson in particular reverted to the theme of parochialism time and again. Here is a characteristic passage from one of his annual reports: "Over-intellectualization, over-specialization, indifference to what other people do for their living, provincialism and narrow sympathies, — all these are, I will not say always facts, but dangers that have to be guarded against in senior boys at Public Boarding schools."

What prompted Leeson's observation was his strong feeling about the benefits boys derived from having to work in the fields during the Second War, planting potatoes and rearing pigs, sharing the lot of the rest of the beleaguered population. Without the war there was always a danger of "thinking and acting as if the life of the school was in some sense an end in itself". Leeson's predecessors had tended to perpetuate the divisions between their pupils and the town. It was regarded as a matter of reproach in 1875 that the "nondescript garments" worn by certain Commoner juniors made it impossible to distinguish them from the ordinary town boy except by "a certain air of refinement". In 1888 the Headmaster refused permission to use the football pitches at Bar End "as he did not wish the School to mix with the town". It was perfectly acceptable for townspeople to show their interest in the school by coming to hear the list of cricket colours announced, or by escorting victorious teams from the station in triumph, but that was about as far as the contact went.

For dons, though insularity within a self-sufficient community was, and still is, a danger, the isolation was not as great. Freddy Morshead served twice as Mayor, and four other members of the staff have followed him in his office; admittedly only one of them was in the last eighty years, but these days it is inconceivable that a Bursar or housemaster should have time, as they did, to combine the mayoralty with their normal work-load. Nonetheless the tradition of service to local government has continued, with dons in the 1980's serving on the City and County Council. So too their more specialized knowledge and experience has long been put to use on behalf of the churches and schools of Winchester.

The boys do not have this sort of opportunity for involvement. For hundreds of years they were not allowed north of the College at all, except on special occasions, and when in 1793 a number of them broke bounds to go and hear a Band Concert in the Cathedral Close a mere stone's throw away, the punishment meted out was so severe that it prompted the worst rebellion in the school's history. Even when the physical restrictions were lifted, it was difficult to find common ground: dress, speech and background helped to keep the two sides apart. Until 1969 boys still had to go into town dressed in the mediaeval cleric's gown, or in a straw hat which seemed old-fashioned even on Inigo Jolliphant's uncle (*The Good Companions*, written sixty years ago). It is not surprising that these outward marks of exclusiveness gave rise to provocation. After a number of ugly clashes the dress rules were relaxed, and now, for better or worse, the universal uniform of jeans

Tea in Chamber Court for the War wounded (1917).

and tee-shirts makes all sorts and conditions of young men virtually indistinguishable.

Combined activities got off to a tentative start with a series of joint debates involving the W.E.A. in the 1920's. Sporting links with local clubs and schools had to wait a little longer. In 1950 an attempt to start a cricket team to play neighbouring villages was scotched, and not for another fifteen years did Senior Club, a team of dons and boys, come into being for this purpose. *The Wykehamist* could still claim in 1947 that Town and Gown were completely isolated except in music. The building of the P.E. Centre in 1969 opened up many more possibilities: unfamiliar sports like basketball, volleyball, and judo grew rapidly, and for competitive purposes there was suitable opposition ready to hand in the other Winchester secondary schools. The more established games have done something to follow this lead, and though most of the major fixtures will continue to be against other independent boarding schools, participation in competitions like the Holt and Gawthorne Trophies for junior cricket teams in Hampshire has shown at least that the school does not regard itself as "above that sort of thing."

Much more significant however, in terms of community relations, was the institution in 1963 of the A.S.A. scheme — Alternative Service Activities — for the employment of those who chose not to join a now voluntary Cadet Force. Boys in the second half of their time at school may now opt to spend an afternoon a week visiting or gardening for old people, providing entertainments for Homes and Day Centres, talking to patients in the geriatric or mental hospital, helping with play groups for infants or handicapped children, or other activities of this kind. There is no need to volunteer for this service: there are other options open, for agricultural, constructional, technical, or clerical work, and the motives guiding their choice are not always very elevated. But many boys do choose to take on a social responsibility, and in doing so benefit themselves as well as the local community.

Of course it is no new thing this social sense. The missionary zeal of the Victorians did not pass Winchester by. A stirring lecture in December 1875 by Robert Linklater on the miseries of London's East End led to

War work: members of the school harvest their potatoes (1917).

Photograph: M.J. Rendall

the inauguration of a Mission there the following year. The palpable evidence of its achievement was the building of a church at East India Dock, but because of the distance the school could give little more than encouragement and money, and when the missioner Mr. Donne decided to move to Limehouse in 1882 this was taken as an opportunity to find a mission-site closer to home.

So began the school's long association with Portsmouth. The pathfinder was again Linklater, who arrived in Portsea that Advent Sunday with nothing but a parcel of books and a box of flea powder. There was no church, not even a house for him to live in; but in spite of a dispiriting start when he was jeered and abused, he soon had people queuing up to join his Sunday School classes, Mothers Meetings, Night Schools, Bible groups, Confirmation classes, and a Working Men's Club. Almost at once he was able to make plans for building a proper church. The fund-raising opened with a concert in Stafford House patronised by the Gladstones; a collection in the school raised the remarkable sum of £100, and one of the housemasters gave up his boarding house in order to work with the Mission. But legal difficulties arose over land-purchase, and it was not until 1898 that the new church of St. Agatha's was consecrated. Occasional visits by boys gave the idea of a Mission some substance for them, and the effect may be represented by this brief letter of the poet Lionel Johnson, whose unusual sensibilities were already apparent at the age of 17: "I have been at Landport, Portsmouth, last Sunday, among the School Mission: a strange experience: Sunday classes, talks with boys of 18, etc.: ritualistic adorabilities: clubs, vespers, teas, all deliciously real: a veritable revelation of real work." But not many had the opportunity to sample these realities, and for the rest the Mission meant little more than the odd sermon with a collection to follow.

A new incumbent brought new life and involvement. Bob Dolling was a remarkable person, of a magnanimity that fully matched his enormous girth. Though a poor man himself — he had to pawn his watch for a night's lodging when he went to be interviewed for his appointment as Missioner — he worked untiringly to raise money for the district. With this he paid for the building of a school, an orphanage, a Mission Hall, and St. Agatha's itself; he purchased the house that contained the last brothel in the area (the rest he had shamed the landlords into evicting); and for years he kept open house, and a common dinner table where the needy could always get a proper meal. Wykehamists coming to stay could find themselves in the company of tramps and prostitutes, an unnerving experience for a sheltered adolescent; but many who later devoted themselves to charity work have testified that their first inspiration came from the Landport Mission.

Dolling's valuable ministry was cut short after eleven years by a liturgical dispute with the new Bishop of Winchester (Portsmouth did not yet have its own diocese). His churchmanship had always been so high as to be virtually indistinguishable from Catholicism, and the conflict came to a head in 1895 over an additional altar designed for the new church: it was to be sited in the south aisle for use in saying Masses for the Dead. The Bishop objected and refused to issue a licence for the church if the altar remained dedicated to that purpose. Dolling would not compromise, and immediately tendered his resignation. He had massive popular support and there was a strong feeling of outrage at his treatment. As a boy in the school naively expressed it: "In as much as he has succeeded in hooking the weak-minded and impressionable into morality by pomps and rituals outside the orthodox church, I hold that he is more than justified in breaking all narrow trammels . . . The whole population, who justly and naturally adore him, as he is a magnificent personality, will rise like a man, and oppose the unfortunate successor who is sent by the Bear (Fearon) and Bishop to remove the altar. Furthermore the whole Mission is dependent on Dolling's personality, so the Bishop, while performing a very obvious duty in his capacity as bishop, will be undoing the splendid work of ten years."

When Dolling left Portsmouth he went first to America, but he never found a similar vocation and died in 1902. The Mission did not, as predicted, die with his departure, nor was his successor frozen out; but the resulting awkwardness contributed to the feeling that, with St. Agatha's now established, it was time to move to another area of Portsmouth. In 1908 Rudmore became the centre for the Mission's operation, and the whole process began again.

The school has been extremely fortunate in its choice of Missioners. Bertie Lucas gave up a comfortable tutorship at Oxford to begin the work at Rudmore from a disused shop. Like Linklater he had to contend with initial suspicion and hostility, and even when, after a successful appeal, a new church to St. John the Baptist was built and consecrated eight years later, the procession from the Mission Hall was greeted with mockery and derision. But Lucas was cheerfully imperturbable, and by living on equal terms with his parishioners (it was said that he knew them all by name, and his speech was heavily infected with the Portsmouth accent) he won their love and trust; Wykehamists too responded readily to the moving and humorous accounts of his stewardship which he gave in School every year, with stories of the prolific Mrs. Bumstead and others of his flock attaining near-legendary status.

His successors, Guy Hanbury and Norman Coley, maintained the momentum, and were directly responsible for bringing many Wykehamists face to face with the realities of working-class life for the first time. The Second War was a time of particular hardship in Portsmouth: St. John's church was among the many buildings hit by German bombs, and remained roofless for ten years. But the coming of the Welfare State and changes in the make-up of Portsmouth's population called into question the

Bob Dolling (centre front) with the men's party from Landport (1893). The gate behind was given in memory of Herbert Stewart (see p.145) and has since been moved round the corner of the Cloisters.

continuance of an enterprise which might look to some suspiciously paternalistic. The Bishop of Portsmouth wrote in 1959: "If Dolling were alive today he would freely admit that it was easier for him — in those days the poor needed help, the ignorant wanted education, young people clamoured for clubs, and Winchester was proud to help Dolling provide for those who could not provide for themselves. But today things are different — what our society needs now is not so much that the fortunate and clever should help the humble and simple, as that people who grow up in different social circumstances should understand and value one another and learn to work together as only Christians can."

The following year, when Coley retired, the old Portsmouth Mission came to an end, and a wholly new approach was tried. Leigh Park was once an area of farm and parkland a few miles north of Havant. In 1947 development of the site began for a future Garden City or New Town; but soon after the first families had moved in, the Government decided that it should simply be an overspill for Portsmouth rather than an independent township. Now its population is around 40,000 making it one of the largest housing estates in Western Europe, with all the social problems of a rootless, isolated community which does not have enough amenities.

This was the object of the latest Winchester College Mission, or as the locals preferred to call it the Winchester Link; the school now gave its support to a team ministry already appointed by the diocese, and no longer installed its own Missioner. Boys continued to be involved in visits — the youth club "Point Seven" provided a useful meeting ground — and in sporting fixtures; but it must be admitted that most of the contact was at a more official level, between the Mission Committee and the ministry, and the boys could not establish more than a tenuous connection during their schooldays. So after 25 years both sides were ready to break the tie.

There was still an outlet for voluntary work in London. When in 1937 the Mission Committee had finally paid off all that was owed for the Church and Hall built at Rudmore, it found itself with a financial surplus for the first time. It seemed a good thing to use this to give official backing to the work begun in Hoxton ten years before by three boys who had just left the school. In 1926, following in the wake of a movement which saw the foundation of the N.A.B.C., and the Duke of York's camps, they started a boys' club at Ely Place, dignified by the name of the Crown Club in 1930, when they acquired the premises of a disused pub. In 1939 when this was taken over by the L.C.C. the Old Etonian trustees of Hoxton Manor gave them a yet larger building, and so the Crown and Manor Club came into being. The founders, Harold Llewellyn Smith and his brother Arthur, an architect whose talent for draughtsmanship was first evident in the caricatures of his teachers at school, devoted much of their lives to the club, and inspired a succession of younger Wykehamists to give their time, interest and energy to the same cause. The needs of the Hoxton community have changed in sixty years, but the value of the club is undiminished.

The call to missionary work does not sound as loudly as it used to. No longer does the young man respond to the promptings of his conscience by forsaking all for the priesthood and plunging into the urban slums to spread the gospel of redemption. Such individual heroics have been squeezed out by the cumbrous state machinery of social welfare. But even if poverty, starvation, and endemic disease are no longer urgent problems in today's Britain, there is still hardship and unhappiness, and it is well that the modern Wykehamist should have some first hand knowledge of it through the A.S.A. organisation, and well that the Mission still operates in Hoxton, providing a focus for those who wish to commit themselves to more of such work after leaving school.

A.S.A. is not for everyone. The alternative is the Combined Cadet Force, notionally a choice between social and military service — or public service, as the current C.C.F. Regulations put it — though few boys would see it in those terms. The idea of serving King, Country and Empire was probably a significant factor in encouraging boys to join the Corps only when war itself threatened: in 1899 when the numbers reached a new peak, and 1914 when for obvious reasons everyone signed up.

Strictly speaking the Corps has never been compulsory, even though for most of the century it has been treated as if it was. It began life in 1860 simply as a volunteer Rifle Club, entirely managed by boys. Shooting was its main concern, and teams competed annually for the inter-schools Ashburton Shield — except in 1866 when a boy was killed by one of his fellows who did not know that the musket he was pointing at him was loaded. Arms drill soon became a part of the Club's activities, and in 1868 it was enrolled as a Cadet Corps in the 1st Hants Volunteer Battalion, with the Second Master George Richardson taking over command.

In 1908 school cadet forces were properly integrated for the first time by the establishment of the Officer Training Corps. In order to accommodate the new schedules, whose end was an exam for passing "Certificate A" the school set aside one teaching hour a week; but it was still possible not to join the Corps if you did not mind doing some extra work instead.

From 1914 onward, with the War Office insisting on regular training for senior cadets, virtually everyone became a member. Even after the War most boys continued to join because they felt, for one reason or another, that it was the thing to do. Conscientious objection was countenanced but rare. However in the late 1920's and 30's when the cry of Disarmament was making itself heard throughout the land, some palliative was provided for the anti-militarists by the formation of a Scouts Troop which was open to anyone over 17.

During the Second War sensitivity about class and rank led to a government pronouncement that every O.T.C. was hereinafter to be called the J. (for Junior) T.C., even though its activities were to remain the same, and its main function was still seen as preparing boys for Officer responsibilities (the eagle eye of Field Marshal Montgomery could detect, so he claimed when he inspected the Contingent in 1946, "latent leadership in all ranks"). The war also gave a separate identity to sections training for entry to the Navy and Air Force, and in order to retain them, the Corps became a Combined Cadet Force in 1948. Such it has remained ever since, though in 1970 one unit of the combination was lopped off, when the Naval section finally ran aground; now it has a Marines section instead.

Until it ended in 1960, National Service provided enough justification for maintaining the element of compulsion; only in Harold Walker's house did the boys, by unilateral declaration, join a year later than the rest —

one of the last grand gestures of housemasterly independence. The wind of change was felt earlier at Winchester than most schools, and in 1963 a genuinely voluntary Corps was introduced, with A.S.A. as the other option. There was no mass desertion from the ranks, and a more streamlined organization has operated very effectively ever since.

The training that could be undertaken by the Corps was severely limited by the fact that until 1939 the only time available for parades was a brief period before lunch. This was too short for anything except practising drills: the tactical exercises, which provided the sole opportunity for developing initiative and other desirable qualities of leadership, were restricted to occasional Field Days and an annual camp.

Field Days are recorded from as early as 1872, when the contingent would march out to do battle with other companies of the 1st Hants on Teg Down. They might have been more popular had they not tended to coincide with Leave-out Days. In 1884, and for about seventy-five years thereafter, there were joint operations with other schools. These provided marvellous opportunities for the Officers who drafted the orders to exercise donnish ingenuity in combining the literary with the ludicrous; a characteristic example begins "According to trustworthy information from Intelligence OLYMPUS, HELEN has left TROY under a smoke-screen and has taken refuge at CRAB WOOD FARM. . .". But for the participants, who usually saw little of the action and understood less, and whose minds were largely taken up with mischevious ideas for diversion, the value could not be reckoned great. Let one memoir stand for many; the fact that it comes from a Field Marshal and Chief of Defence Staff, whose own career in the Winchester Corps had been by no means illustrious, gives it added piquancy. "My memories of the Corps are restricted to some of the more unorthodox incidents. To one member of the house swallowing worms for money to while away the boredom of manning a defensive position near Amphitheatre: to participating in a section raid led by my elder brother which captured Wellington's bugler and forced him to blow the Exercise End call with awkward results to all of us, and to sending the Second Master on his horse galloping madly across the Aldershot training area by use of that not very secret weapon, a pencil propelled from the rifle by a round of blank".

In 1939 the Commanding Officer, Jack Parr, won from the school authorities permission to use one afternoon a week for training in addition to the morning drill parades. This greatly enlarged the scope and effectiveness of the instruction, though whether it served to prepare boys any better for the realities of armed conflict is open to doubt. The Leopard Crawl, the Gliding Blob (a formation for crossing roads in the dark), the night-glasses (opaque goggles to simulate the very pitch of night on a blazing July afternoon), the Right Flanking section attack, the burnt cork for blacking faces, the indestructible haversack rations, the potassium permanganate in

N.C.O.'s of the Rifle Corps (1879).

the waterbottles — all these were part of the elaborate game of military training, which most boys were prepared to play with energy, patience, cunning and good humour, because like many activities it was only worth doing if you were prepared to take trouble over it.

Nothing exemplified more clearly the ritualistic, non-real nature of this training than Platoon Battle Drill. This was a formalised representation of a platoon attack, carried out in conditions as far removed from noise, the smell, the fear, and the disorder of battle as it would be possible to invent. In their best uniforms on a flat area of playing-field, the platoon trotted through a rigidly ordered series of movements with much lifting of the knees, and rifles held at the excruciating High Port position. With economic symbolism words supplied the place of action: standing with parade-ground fixity the combatants registered their reactions to enemy attack by chanting, in well rehearsed unison, "Down, Crawl, Observe, Sights, Fire!" A feint to the right, and then a disciplined charge with (imaginary) bayonets fixed. Bloodless victory accomplished over the non-existent enemy, the platoon regrouped with further cries of "Casualties — Ammunition — Administration and Logistics" and then left the field for another squad to go through the same gyrations.

Platoon Battle Drill was, I believe, discontinued in the Army in 1943. It was practised at Winchester until March 1958 when its obsequies were performed with fitting ceremony.

Of course, the Corps should not be judged by its use of drills that bear no more relation to real warfare than the Japanese Noh theatre. Winchester's military record in the two World Wars is impressive (see p.182); but there is no evidence to show that this stemmed from proficiency in the school contingent, and certainly none of our eminent war-leaders — Wavell, Dowding, and Portal — seems to have made any sort of mark in the ranks of the Corps. The conclusion to be drawn is not that the C.C.F., or its earlier equivalents, is inefficient or a waste of time; but that its function should be seen in educational rather than strictly military terms. These words written by Jack Parr, who was associated with it for virtually all the first half of the century, will serve as well as any to define its purpose " . . . to eliminate self-consciousness . . . and to inculcate self-confidence, self-control, poise, and the elements of discipline, decent behaviour, and a sense of responsibility." This remains as true today as it was fifty or even a hundred years earlier: what has changed is the way in which these ends are pursued.

When the Corps went voluntary in 1963 under the command of Digby Grist, its first C.O. from the Regular Army, it was already broadening the base of its operations to include more "adventurous training" of the kind that Field Marshal Templer had recently been recommending. There was a Self-Reliance section, which had the pleasure of camping out on the night before a big Field Day (sausages over the camp fire, and clandestine forays to the pub down the road), ambushing the drowsy opposition as they got out of their coaches next morning, and then going home for the day; there were courses in First Aid, Woodmanship, and Civil Defence; the first Greenfields camp was organized, when the school contingent got away from the great tented armies of Tidworth Pennings or Buckenham Tofts, and ran its own exercises from the privacy of a Welsh mountain valley.

Since Robin Somerset, formerly of the Royal Green Jackets which is now the C.C.F's parent unit, took over command in 1969, the process has gone much further, and the Winchester Corps has played a substantial part in piloting the syllabus which the Ministry of Defence has now accepted for its Army Proficiency Certificate (APEX, replacing Cert.A.). This is how it works. There is one compulsory year when boys learn the rudiments of drill, and other more practical things like campcraft and map-reading. Then those who decide to join the C.C.F. proper rather than the A.S.A. undertake a series of courses, some compulsory, some optional; passes in five of these courses, which range from shooting to night-patrolling to canoeing, qualify a cadet for his certificate. Members of the R.A.F. section are integrated into the same system, but have some of their own courses specially leading to R.A.F. Proficiency; for them the great attraction is that

A pre-war Field Day operation on Twyford Down.

with the right qualities they can also learn to pilot a glider or even a powered aeroplane while still at school.

Wednesday afternoon parades are designed to promote certain skills, either technical, like using radio transmitters, or managerial — instructing others or making decisions. Some of these are put into practice in the termly overnight exercises, which involve map-reading, camping, and various forms of battlecraft. But the ultimate test, where the training has to be put to use in real rather than simulated situations, is provided at the annual camps: one of fifty or sixty boys in the summer, often held among the northern hills, and a smaller mountaineering or canoeing camp at Easter. Here the difficulties of terrain and weather provide genuine challenges for boys to meet — at different levels according to their age, strength, and experience. When a leader can safely bring his party through the rapids of the Wye or over the snowy crags of Scafell and Great Gable, then he will have achieved something substantial as well as satisfying.

At a time when other branches of school life no longer feature so strongly the traditional notions of responsibility and discipline, the modern C.C.F. has a more extensive educational role to play than it did when all its activities were military. Its appeal is still strong — in some years it attracts more volunteers than the A.S.A. — and this may be due to the non-military accent of much of the training. The lure of a heavily subsidised week in the Western Highlands, the Peak District, the Cheviots or the Wye Valley is incentive enough for many. But it would be wrong to imagine the C.C.F. as simply a form of Outward Bound School. The mock-battles between BRUTE Force and KREWD Force on Exercise Spring Fever are fought out with as much relish as the War-Games of which they are an extension; and there is a steady stream of applicants for commissions in the Armed Services.

Winchester is not a military school and never has been. Even in 1914 when so many activities were suddenly being channelled into the war effort, the Headmaster was able to say "I am not at all afraid of any spirit of militarism at Winchester: other influences are too strong." Much more is this true in peacetime. With the enlightened and generous support of the Ministry of Defence, the Corps should continue to be fun while still fulfilling its official aims of helping to develop "discipline, endurance, resourcefulness, self-reliance, and leadership . . . things that are of profound consequence to the stamina and stability of the nation, in peace as well as in war."

Lessons in watermanship with the modern C.C.F. (1973).
(Below) as you make your own raft, so shall you lie on it – or under it.

Recruits' Rifle Drill (1952).   *Photograph: Eric Auerbach*

Chapter X

Wykehamists of Fact And Fiction

James Bond, secret agent 007, is off on another of his cloak-and-dagger missions to Berlin. In the musty lobby of the rendezvous he meets his chaperon, Captain Paul Sender, late of the Welsh Guards, "a lean, tense man in his early forties" who is dressed in "the uniform of his profession — well-cut, well-used light-weight tweeds in a dark green herringbone, a soft white silk shirt and an old school tie — in this case, Wykehamist. At the sight of the tie . . . Bond's spirits, already low, sank another degree. He knew the type: backbone of the Civil Service, overcrammed and underloved at Winchester, a good Second in P.P.E. at Oxford; the war, staff jobs he would have done meticulously, perhaps an O.B.E. . . ."

Captain Sender is only one of the dozens of Wykehamist characters who appear in fiction. The game of identifying them was started by Ronald Hamilton in an article for *The Trusty Servant* (December 1962), and pursued for another year and more as correspondents, further encouraged by the columnist William Hickey, raised the tally to fifty. Even now they continue to pop up from time to time: the earliest recorded is Peregrine Pickle, Smollett's eponymous hero (1751), and among the more recent of note are two characters in Iris Murdoch's *The Sea, the Sea* (1978). Winchester has, let us be thankful, been largely spared the full fictional treatment. The only serious attempt was made in 1935 by E.H. Lacon-Watson's *In the Days of his Youth*, a recreation of the school of fifty years earlier under Ridding (thinly disguised as Dr. Spedding). Contemporary reviews were cool in their praises, and its subsequent disappearance from public notice has made nonsense of the publisher's claim that it could stand comparison with any school story since *Tom Brown's Schooldays*. Nevertheless the regularity with which Wykehamist figures are used in fiction suggests that there are certain attributes of character or accomplishment which the reading public can associate with a Winchester education. What happens if we try to place these literary conceptions alongside the factual record of Wykehamist careers and achievements?

Let us go back to Captain Paul Sender — a meticulous, unobtrusive, charmless Civil Servant. Lord Bognor (*Some People* by Harold Nicolson) is a bigger version of the same: impeccable in his dress, his manner, his friends; with a sound intellect and an excellent memory (he also gets "a very good second" at Oxford), well balanced mentally and morally, he is a paragon of the British Diplomatic Corps, but at the same time soulless, bland, removed from reality. Lawrence Durrell produces two other Foreign Office Wykehamists, Errol the diligent but dull, "goat-like" Head of Chancery in *Mountolive,* and in *Espirit de Corps* Antrobus, portentous and serious-minded, whose face and fingers are constantly working in agonies of self-expression.

The Wykehamist Civil Servant seems to have achieved the status of a stereotype. "In the mythology of the English upper class" wrote Geoffrey Hodgson in a *Sunday Times* colour magazine, "The Wykehamist is not the Cabinet Minister, but his permanent under-secretary; not the general, but his chief of staff . . .". The substance upon which this myth is founded is slight. What the Wykehamist actually does with his life has been minutely researched by two past members of the school, T.J.H. Bishop and R.H. Wilkinson. Their tables, which cover all traceable Wykehamists born between 1820 and 1922 show that during that century only about one Wykehamist in every fourteen entered Government service of any kind. Since then the number has steadily diminished: nowadays it is more like one in fifty.

It is true however that Wykehamists have often risen high in this profession. Besides Warren Fisher who was head of the Civil Service before the last war, there have been plenty of K.C.M.G.'s and permanent under-secretaries (did Lawrence Durrell know of Sir Reginald Antrobus who was Senior Crown Agent for the Colonies in 1909-18?); in the last thirty years there have been Wykehamist Ambassadors in Paris, Moscow, and Washington, and there are still a number of capitals around the world where the monitoring devices of other nations could be baffled by exchanging information in the language of Winchester "notions".

The Civil Service myth keeps company with the myth of the socialist politician. Two fictional Wykehamists (in *The Enormous Shadow* by Robert Harling and *The Blue Field* by Maurice Halliday) are Labour M.P's — one is actually a Communist who defects to the Russians — and Michael Mont of *The Forsyte Saga* is suspected of being "a sort of socialist".

In fact Winchester has never been a school much connected with politics. The only Wykehamist Prime Minister, Henry Addington, is remembered only for his insignificance beside William Pitt. There have been one or two other near misses: Disraeli's elder brothers were Wykehamists, and he might have come to the school himself but for a delicate constitution; Hugh Gaitskell seemed set for the premiership when a viral infection caused his untimely death. But never during this century have there been more than fifteen

Wykehamist M.P's at one time in the Commons, and most of them have been Conservative. There was one Wykehamist socialist elected in 1922, five in the great Labour sweep of 1945, and just one or two in every Parliament since 1966. In the 1979 Conservative administration there were three Wykehamist Cabinet Ministers, as there were under Churchill (1951-54) and Gladstone (1872-4).

In spite of these figures it is the socialist politicians from Winchester whose names are remembered. The intellectual qualities of men like Stafford Cripps, Gaitskell, and Crossman raised them to high positions in their party, at a time when a commitment to socialism did not entail erasing from *Who's Who* references to one's Public School education. Since the leadership of Harold Wilson, whose experience at Oxford gave him a rooted dislike of the Wykehamist intellectual, and the growth of influence exercised by the extreme Left, the phenomenon of Winchester Socialism has almost, but not quite, disappeared.

In the school itself opinion has always been overwhelmingly conservative, reflecting largely the politics of parents who would choose and could afford to send their children to such a place. Mock elections have usually been a walkover for the right-wing candidates, except in the anarchic days of 1970 when the Mad Hatter's Tea Party swept all before it. But intellectual independence has always been encouraged and practised, and it is not at all surprising that between the wars the consciousness of a need for social changes led a small but prominent minority to espouse the ideals of socialism, when membership of the Labour Party seemed to offer the best hope of achieving them.

———————

Around the turn of the century a pamphlet was published on "Where we get our best men"; it examined the origins of men who had risen to prominence in Victoria's reign. The Public Schools as a whole provided 30% of the eminent, and 37% of the pre-eminent: most of them were in Government and the professions, whereas the contribution to Science was small, and to Art negligible. Winchester was not particularly well represented, holding only fifth place among individual schools. An editorial in *The Wykehamist* summed up: "In relation to other schools our best achievements are in Law and the Church. In Literature, Science, Government, and the Press our contribution is miserably small; while to Medicine, Diplomacy, Philanthropy, and Art we contribute nothing. Considered proportionally our only passable performances are in Government Service and Society, in which we have produced 7% of all those who have attained eminence. Neither of these callings, it will be admitted, demand any remarkable degree of intellectual brilliancy."

The Church was at one time (c.1840-50) attracting about one Wykehamist in every three: the fathers of nearly half the boys in the school were themselves ordained. Parental example was then a major influence in determining a boy's career, and T.J.H. Bishop's figures show a close correlation between the occupations of fathers and sons. During this century fewer and fewer people in the Church have been able to afford Winchester fees; and there has been a corresponding drop in the number of boys themselves seeking ordination. In 1930 there were nine Wykehamist Bishops at the Lambeth Conference; today there are still about a hundred Wykehamists in Holy Orders, but the Bishops reduced to one, the Suffragan of Warwick.

In literature Wykehamist clerics are represented by the Rev. Francis Arabin, the agreeable and cultivated vicar of St. Ewold, formerly Professor of Poetry at Oxford, who ends up as Dean of Barchester, and by the nice but ineffectual John Wentworth in *The Rosemary Tree* by Elizabeth Goudge.

The Law has always been one of the most popular professions for Wykehamists, and it is strange that more Winchester lawyers do not occur in fiction. Nicholas Monsarrat's John Morrell is one, and he looks distressingly like another out of the Civil Service mould: a meticulous dresser, and "a living reproof to the solecism of displaying emotion" he had been a junior barrister before the war involved him in the relentless hardships of *The Cruel Sea*. Another example is Gaskony, the retired Judge in *The Judge's Story* by Charles Morgan. On average ten Wykehamists go into the Law every year, and Winchester has for generations been better represented in the Judiciary than any other school. On a famous occasion in 1937 seven Wykehamist High Court Judges were received *Ad Portas* (see p.154); the number has been even higher since then (ten in 1939), and the ceremony was repeated with nine judges in 1981 (see p.iv).

The pamphlet of 1900 makes no mention of Wykehamists in the Forces. This may seem odd when so many boys were going into the army every year. Yet it does appear to be the case that the highest ranks remained out of their reach: in World War I 2214 Wykehamists were on active service, but none rose higher than Lieutenant General. Since then there have been several Wykehamist Field Marshals and Air Marshals, and the *Sunday Times* contention that the Wykehamist was "not the General but the chief of staff" brought an indignant riposte from the keeper of the records, claiming that there were 43 Old Wykehamists, active or retired, who had the seniority of at least a Major General. Nor would there be much truck with James Bond's sneer about wartime O.B.E's: in 1914-18 there were 44 O.B.E's won, to 4 V.C's, 320 M.C's, and 214 D.S.O's; in 1939-45 128 M.C's, 26 D.S.O's, 26 D.S.C's and 29 D.F.C's, to 84 O.B.E's. These days there is less attraction in service life, apart from University cadetships and short

The War Cloister designed by Herbert Baker to commemorate the 500 Wykehamist dead of the 1914-1918 War.

Photograph: Richard Shorter

service commissions, and it may be some time before there are again, as there were in 1980, two Wykehamist full generals serving concurrently.

The Wykehamist soldiers in fiction, and there are plenty of them, are a varied and interesting bunch. We start with Viscount Castlewood from *Henry Esmond,* a lively buccaneering spirit upon whom a year's education at "the famous college" near his Hampshire home appears to have had passing little effect; then a fine pair of stiff-upper-lipped heroes in one of P.C. Wren's Foreign Legion stories; and so on through nearly a dozen others to General Sir James Arrowby in *The Sea The Sea.* Arrowby is as complex as any of Iris Murdoch's major characters, a scholar with a gift for languages and mathematics as well as winning history prizes, a poet, traveller, connoisseur, a Buddhist convert, a mystic with apparently supernatural powers, who is ultimately able to will his own death. He represents another Winchester type, the man of action whose keenness of mind is combined with unusual sensitivity, a man who becomes a hero in spite of his natural inclinations, while still preserving a certain cool detachment. A model for this figure might be found in Frank Thompson, poet, Communist, and Slavophile, who was parachuted into Yugoslavia in 1944 to help the Bulgarian resistance movement, and some months later died in front of a firing squad giving the salute of freedom. The railway station at Prokopnik is still named after him.

In the last century, we were told, Wykehamists contributed virtually nothing to the Arts. The writers of the pamphlet must have forgotten about Anthony Trollope, or perhaps they did not regard him as a Wykehamist because his stay in the school was short and apparently unhappy. Certainly it was a difficult time for his family and his elder brother Thomas Adolphus may have been particularly unkind to him. But it is significant that he portrays Wykehamists sympathetically in his novels, Arthur Wilkinson and George Bertram in *The Bertrams* as well as Francis Arabin; and in his last, unfinished, book *The Landleaguers* Winchester is the haven which Philip seeks for his obstinate son Florian.

Still Trollope was an exception, and the general charge of cultural aridity was merited. That deficiency has been to some extent made up since. But it is indicative of the emphasis of Winchester education that more have made their mark as critics than as creators. Admittedly the articulation of aesthetic judgements was raised by Kenneth Clark to an art-form in itself. But there are no Wykehamist artists to match him in distinction. There is instead a thin but enduring line of experts in different specialities of the art world — advisers to the great auctioneering firms, keepers of museum departments and the like. In the literary world Wykehamists become journalists (even Editors of *The Times*) rather than novelists. In music the critics and administrators outnumber the composers and concert-soloists. Of Jack Toye's sons one became music critic for *The Morning Post,* to be

Defending the North West frontier: Maj.-Gen. H.L. Haughton, (left) with Sir Richard Maconachie and Sikander Khan – and Chieftain the golden retriever, near Kabul (1936).

followed by Martin Cooper and John Warrack of *The Daily Telegraph*, William Mann of *The Times*, and David Cairns of *The Sunday Times*; the other became Managing Director of Covent Garden Opera. In 1948 the head of the Music Department of the B.B.C., and the Directors of both Opera and Ballet at Sadlers Wells were all Wykehamists, and later that tradition was maintained by Robert Irving who is reckoned to have conducted more performances of ballet than anyone else alive. Madrigalists will know the

A print of c.1890 suggestive of Winchester's

c, athletic, and social ideals at the time.

name of Cecil Armstrong Gibbs, lovers of *musique concrète* acknowledge
the expertise of Humphrey Searle; otherwise there have been no Wykehamist
composers of established reputation.

Actors there have been in surprising numbers, though few since the
days of F.R. Benson have been at the top of the profession. Anthony Asquith
is by some way the best known film-director, but in the film festivals around
the world one or two others are currently making a name for themselves.
Apart from them there is, among younger Wykehamists, just a handful making
a living out of their artistic talents — a violinist, a potter, a singer or two,
a few artists, designers, and architects. It may be some years yet before
the careers of Wykehamists reflect the greater emphasis currently being given
to creative activities within the school.

In the Sciences medicine has always had a strong following: even a
hundred years ago, when very little science was being taught, it was attracting
about 5% of all leavers, a figure not reached again until the 1960's. Most
are doctors, a few are vets, and Dorothy Sayers (*In the Teeth of the Evidence*)
conjured up a Wykehamist dentist for Lord Peter Wimsey, one Mr.
Lamplough. Engineering was for a long time comparable in popularity with
medicine, and it is disconcerting to find that since 1945, when the demand
and opportunities for engineers have expanded so much, there have actually
been fewer boys following that course. In other branches of Science one
can point to teachers and researchers all over the world, to a galaxy of
F.R.S's, and indeed to one Nobel Prize winner.

In fact in almost every field of intellectual endeavour there are likely
to be found Wykehamist names. Some of the greatest mathematicians of
the century have come from Winchester: G.H. Hardy, author of the classic
Mathematician's Apology as well as more severe treatises on Pure Mathematics;
F.P. Ramsey, who had already written *The Foundations of Mathematics* before
his death at the age of 26; and perhaps one might add Rollo Davidson
who was only 25 and already a pioneer with an international reputation
in certain fields of Probability and Statistics when a climbing accident on
the Piz Bernina ended his life in 1970; Freeman Dyson, son of the former
Master of Music, who took a chair at Princeton in his twenties and came
to be reckoned a second Einstein; and, from the same remarkable College
Election Roll of 1936, James Lighthill, now the doyen of British
mathematicians.

In Classics and Archaeology the roll of honour goes back to H. Furneaux,
the editor of Tacitus; F.J. Haverfield, one of the great Romano-British scholars
of the last century; and F.G. Kenyon, President of the British Academy
and Doctor of ten Universities. They were followed by R. W. Livingstone,
A.E. Zimmern, the Myres father and son, J.D. Denniston of *The Greek
Particles*, J.D.S. Pendlebury of Crete, and C.F.C. Hawkes. Now the stars
of the new generation are already rising (mention has been made of some

of them on page 136). I have omitted from the list Arnold Toynbee, who deserves a category of his own, as does H.A.L. Fisher who rose to Cabinet office as well as being one of the most widely read of all historians. Both were trained in the Classics.

The academic world is still well peopled with Wykehamists, and there is no particular bias evident in their choice of subjects. There have, in recent years, been Professors of every branch of Science from Theoretical Mechanics to Orthopaedic Surgery, from Psychology to Oceanography; of Classics, Mathematics, Law, English, History, Economics, and Divinity; of Social Anthropology, European Archaeology, International Relations, and Semitic Philology; of Drama, Music, and Art. There have been Heads of Colleges, including two Wardens of All Souls, and Vice-Chancellors of Universities.

The intellectual prowess of the Wykehamist is one of his most widely recognised attributes, even if in truth it is one that applies more to College than to the school as a whole. Some instances from literature have already been noticed and the scholar-aesthete is a favourite type. We might add the names of George Souldern, a double First and University prizewinner, who later becomes "a figure of national importance" in one of Buchan's stories in *The Runagates Club;* Pappenhacker from Evelyn Waugh's *Scoop*, described as "the cleverest man in Fleet Street" who liked playing with a toy train which he would address in Latin Alcaics; G. Odoreida, one of Stephen Potter's most celebrated Lifemen, whose badminton match with the Yugoslav champion Bzo remains a classic of inventiveness; and Merlyn, Wart's tutor, in *The Once and Future King* by T.H. White, with his gold medal for being "the best scholar at Winchester".

It is natural that the teacher should try to stimulate in his pupils the scholarly appetites that have stirred himself, and should encourage them to put the pursuit of knowledge high on their list of objectives. Genius of mind, said Budge Firth, was "one of the only two earthly things before which the young might be allowed, even encouraged to bend their proud heads" (the other was "warmth and benevolence of heart"). To the extent that Winchester masters had higher academic credentials than most, and their pupils had above average intelligence, this did prompt the best brains to devote themselves to a life of scholarship. But what of the boys who were not so gifted or that way motivated, who may not have shared their teachers' enthusiasm for the things of the mind? For distinguished as the ranks of Winchester scholars, real and fictional, may be, they are numerically slight: only five or ten every year go into teaching of any kind. Those who speak in general and often disparaging terms of the Wykehamist's intellectualism, and complain of his lack of worldliness, tend to be blinded by the achievements and attitudes of a small minority. They could do well to reflect on the fact that for the last sixty years at least, since trade and commerce became respectable professions, far more Wykehamists have had careers in Business than in anything else. Of those who came to the school in 1955-60 for instance, well over a third are thus engaged.

There has for years been a Business section in the Old Wykehamist news compiled for the school magazine with devotion, and a good deal of acerbic comment, by the Jacker and latterly by Gerry Dicker. It does not, and could not, constitute a complete record of achievement in so diversified a field, but it can at least provide a corrective to the view that the Wykehamist is only interested in the printed word. Let us take the twenty years or so from 1965. The Business section during that time records the appointment of Wykehamists to the chairmanship of well over a hundred companies. That includes three successive chairmen of Barclay's Bank and two of the Council of the Stock Exchange; chairmen also of Lloyd's Bank and the Westminster Bank, of B.A.C., I.P.C., G.E.C., and the B.B.C.; of Shell, Lever Bros., Tate and Lyle, and the Imperial Group; chairmen of the Monopolies Commission, the Horserace Totalizator Board, the Forestry Commission; chairmen of Cornhill, Sun Alliance, and Lloyd's of London; and Director Generals of the B.B.C. and the National Trust. Sir Denys Lowson, youngest ever Lord Mayor of London, was at one time chairman of over twenty companies, and director of a dozen more. In Banking, Insurance, Publishing, and Brewing Wykehamists seem to have been traditionally prominent; over the last twenty years there has been a strong move into the servicing industries of finance and investment consultancy, with accountancy becoming for the first time a more popular qualification than legal training. Let the Wykehamist's contribution to the nation be judged by these men as much as by the scholars and administrators: but let the business community also be warned by the story of the Wykehamist who was offered the sale of the Catseye patent for £150 — and turned it down.

Schooling is only one of the things that influences a choice of career; home background and the availability of opportunities are in most cases more potent forces. A school is primarily concerned with success in its own context and this does not necessarily have much bearing on success in later life. "It is indeed strange" said Ridding in a sermon of 1870 "how rarely a leading boy becomes a leading man . . . Ordinarily the qualities which win admiration among boys are not those which tell in later life." The same conclusion was reached, rather more painstakingly, by Bishop and Wilkinson, with the one qualification that former Senior Commoner Prefects did seem to get on significantly better in later life.

Members of the Senior Classical Division of 1956, seen here in Meads with J.G. Stow, went on into careers that included Music, Medicine, Computer Programming, Accountancy, Management Consultancy and the Diplomatic Service. *Photograph: Keystone Press*

To include a record of Old Wykehamist achievement in an account of the school's development is to add an appendix that is of considerable interest in itself; but to claim that the successes and failures are directly attributable to the schooling they received is absurd. With most boys going on to further education there has not been the same urgency about fitting them for certain jobs or professions that most schools have. Winchester had no Careers Master until 1947, and only in the last twenty years or so has the guidance given been on a properly organised basis. Before that the advice was as likely to consist of a vague statement of high principle like Fearon's call "to feel, and help others to feel, that money-making and luxurious life are sordid and debasing ends to set before us" or the much repeated admonition to follow a life of service.

There is no such thing as a Wykehamical type outside fiction, and if anyone says that there is, "throw a melon at him" as Alwyn Williams boldly recommended. For every group that seems to conform to a pattern there are plenty of individuals who break the mould: explorers like E.S. Grogan who walked the length of Africa in 1897-1900, and Apsley Cherry Garrard who survived Scott's Antarctic expedition; mountaineers (there were three on the 1921 Everest expedition) and 'circumnavigators; the Boys Own Paper hero A.J. Evans who escaped as a P.O.W. in the First War *and* later played cricket for England; Sir Edmund Backhouse, the great counterfeiter, who persuaded governments to make him their agent for the purchase of millions of pounds of non-existent weapons and bank-notes, even a fleet of phantom battleships; Brian Trubshaw, Chief Test Pilot of Concorde; Richard Noble, successful contender for the world land-speed record; Prison Governors, Horse Trainers, Monks, Inventors, Hippies. What have these in common with each other, and with all the civil servants, clerics, academics, soldiers, scientists, bankers, industrialists, farmers and artists, except for the accident of having been to the same school? Well, perhaps there is something. I think I would accept that, even in the arts and in business, Wykehamists *tend* to be analytical rather than constructive, and that there is a connection between this and the mental disciplines which a Winchester education imposes. But even as I say this I look apprehensively over my shoulder in anticipation of a shower of ambrosial melons thrown from Olympian heights by an episcopal hand.

Winchester in 1982. Pictures of different aspects of life at the College in 1982 on the ensuing six pages are by Willis Wood.

WARDENS OF WINCHESTER COLLEGE

1382	Thomas Cranley	1501	John Rede
1389	John Westcote	1520	Ralph Barnacke
1394	John Morys	1526	Edward More
1413	Robert Thurburn	1542	John White
1450	Thomas Chaundler	1554	John Boxall
1454	John Baker	1556	Thomas Stempe
1488	Michael Cleve	1581	Thomas Bilson

1596	John Harmar
1613	Nicholas Love
1630	John Harris
1658	William Burt
1679	John Nicholas
1712	Thomas Braithwaite
1720	John Cobb
1724	John Dobson
1730	Henry Bigg
1740	John Coxed
1757	Christopher Golding
1763	Harry Lee
1789	George Isaac Huntingford
1832	Robert Speckott Barter
1861	Godfrey Bolles Lee
1904	Kenneth Augustus Muir-Mackenzie
1915	James Parker Smith
1920	William Waldegrave Palmer
1925	Frederic George Kenyon
1930	Frederic John Napier Thesiger
1932	Oswald Richard Arthur Simpkin
1936	Harold Trevor Baker
1946	Gavin Turnbull Simonds
1951	George Henry Gater
1959	Patrick William Duff
1962	Anthony William Tuke
1970	Arthur Lionel Pugh Norrington
1974	Roger Mellor Makins
1978	Austin Richard William (Toby) Low
1987	Christopher Jeremy Morse

HEADMASTERS OF WINCHESTER COLLEGE

1373	Richard Herton
(1388)	John Melton (or Milton)
1394	Thomas Romsey
1407	John Pole
1414	Thomas Romsey
1418	Richard Darcy
1424	Thomas Alwyn (or Walwin)
1430	William Waynflete
1441	Thomas Alwyn (again)
1444	William Ive (or Yve)
1454	John Barnard (or Bernard)
(1459)	John Grene
1465	Clement Smyth
1467	Richard Dene
1484	John Rede
1490	Robert Festham (or Fescam)
1495	William Horman
1501	John Farlyngton (or Farlton)
(1507)	Edward More
1515	Thomas Erlisman
1525	John Twychener (or Towchener)
1531	Richard Twychener (or Tochynar)
1535	John White
1542	Thomas Bayly (or Bailey)
(1547)	William Everard (or Evered)
(1553)	Thomas Hyde
1561	Christopher Johnson
1572	Thomas Bilson
1579	Hugh Lloyd
1588	John Harmar
1596	Benjamin Heyden
1602	Nicholas Love
1613	Hugh Robinson
1627	Edward Stanley
1642	John Potenger (or Pottinger)
1653	William Burt
1658	Henry Beeston
1679	William Harris
1700	Thomas Cheyney
1724	John Burton
1766	Joseph Warton

Headmasters (continued)

1793	William Stanley Goddard
1810	Henry Dyson Gabell
1824	David Williams
1836	George Moberly
1867	George Ridding
1884	William Andrewes Fearon
1901	Hubert Murray Burge
1911	Montague John Rendall
1924	Alwyn Terrell Petre Williams
1934	Spencer Leeson
1946	Walter Fraser Oakeshott
1954	Henry Desmond Pritchard Lee
1968	John Leonard Thorn
1985	James Paley Sabben-Clare

SECOND MASTERS OF WINCHESTER COLLEGE

Between 1388 and 1646 there were about 60 holders of the office of Hostiarius or, as it came to be known, Second Master. As many of the early details are uncertain their names have not been included in this list.

1646	William Ayliffe
1649	Owen Phillips
1678	Benjamin Horne
1701	Thomas Fletcher
1713	Benjamin Wotton
1719	Christopher Eyre
1740	Samuel Speed
1755	Joseph Warton
1766	Thomas Collins
1784	William Stanley Goddard
1793	Henry Dyson Gabell
1810	David Williams
1824	Charles Henry Ridding
1835	Charles Wordsworth
1846	Frederic Wickham
1863	George Ridding
1867	James John Hornby
1868	William Awdry
1873	George Richardson
1899	Montague John Rendall
1911	James Alfred Fort
1916	Alwyn Terrell Petre Williams
1924	Reginald Montague Wright
1952	Thomas Edward Brodie Howarth
1962	Martin Spencer Scott
1979	James Paley Sabben-Clare
1985	Stephen Charles Winkley

APPENDIX 1

Organization of the school in 1861 and 1988

1861		*No. of boys*
Sixth Book	Senior Division	22
	Junior Division	19
Fifth Book	Senior Part	38
	Middle Part, Senior Division	31
	Middle Part, Junior Division	27
	Junior Part	23
Fourth Book	Senior Division	27
	Junior Division	10
TOTAL:	8 divisions for 197 boys	

1988 (number of boys in brackets)

	A Ladder	B Ladder	C Ladder
Sixth Book 1	Senior Div. (16)	4 divs. (60)	3 divs. (46)
Sixth Book 2	Junior Div. (10)	4 divs. (68)	4 divs. (71)

Fifth Book	(Senior Part)	9 divisions (138)

Fourth Book (Middle Part)	8 divisions (127)
(Junior Part)	7 divisions (114)

TOTAL: 650 boys in 41 divisions.

APPENDIX 2

The origins of Domum

The evidence for supposing that *Domum* was composed by a group of scholars, beleaguered on a farm at Crawley by the Plague of 1666 (see p.158 with Stevens *Winton* 1.503 ff.), is circumstantial only, but none the less attractive.

In the absence of any reliable information about the song from external sources, we must rely on what we can glean from the words themselves (see the Latin text on p.117). The first thing that must be said is that the poetry is pretty awful. The verses are of uneven quality, and not even uniform in structure. In the first three there is a rhyme, of a sort, between the short third and fourth lines (*canticum – domum; tedium – omnium; negotium – otium*). In the last three there is not. There are also many infelicities in the language and structure. Take verse five for instance, which has an improper use of *fer* for 'bring' the artificial insertion of *eja,* and an extremely awkward dislocation of word-order in the last two lines with both *ets* misplaced. Again, *Daulias advena* (the visitor from Daulis) is an unhappy circumlocution for 'nightingale' and there is some confusion over *Phosporus,* the morning star, which may be said to 'shine out' *(emicans)* but could hardly boast a *iubar* (sunbeam). The last line is in any case lifted almost wholesale from Martial (Epigrams 8.21): *Phosphore, redde diem; quid gaudia nostra moraris?* And so on.

The whole thing bears the stamp of a schoolboy exercise. But if that accounts for the authorship, what about the date? John Reading who composed the music was organist from 1681 till his death in 1692. The words were evidently not written for him because his tune does not fit the metre. This is seen most clearly in the last line where a very heavy musical stress falls incongruously on the short third syllable. So probably before 1681, but when?

Two little bits of internal evidence help us. One is the reference to *prata* (meadows) which suggests a country setting (it *could* be Meads, but the boys were not officially allowed there yet); and nightingales in Chamber Court are even rarer than in Berkeley Square. The other is the call to Roger to 'bring the horses'. This person can hardly be other than Roger Oades whose name appears very regularly in the Bursar's account-books of the 17th century. He seems to have been a general purpose servant and messenger, mentioned first in the late 1630's cleaning drains and emptying lavatories, then graduating onto the carrying of letters and other less menial jobs. From 1673 he turns up in a different role (unless it is someone else of the same name) as a *firmarius* or farmer, supplying an annual side of bacon to the Fellows.

Roger's ostlering days belong principally to the 1660s, and, coming now to the central piece of evidence, we find among the accounts for the year 1666 entries which show that, because of the Plague, the College rented the farm of one Henry Tamage at Crawley and lodged the boys there 'for the month of Pentecost' (which accounts for the nightingale); compensation had to be paid to the farmer because the boys' games prevented him getting his hay-crop in from the meadow (the *pratum*); and furthermore Roger Oades was paid ten shillings 'for taking the provisions to Crawley'. No wonder the boys were so anxious for him and his pack-animals to arrive! And no wonder they sang of home with such feeling, when Whitsuntide usually brought them a month's holiday!

NOTES AND BIBLIOGRAPHY

Much of the information in this book is drawn from the pages of the school magazine *The Wykehamist* which has been appearing eight or ten times a year since 1866. I am most grateful to the proprietors Messrs. P. and G. Wells of Winchester for permission to use it. In addition I thank the Trustees of Wykehamist Society for allowing me to use material from the old boys magazine *The Trusty Servant* which has been produced twice a year since 1956. References in the notes to these publications, abbreviated to W. and T.S., are given by volume, page and date.

There is an abundance of other primary source material in the College archives, the relevant parts of which are catalogued in *Winchester College Muniments I* (1976) by Sheila Himsworth (abbreviated to W.C.M.), and in the smaller Wiccamica Collection. I am grateful to the Warden and Fellows for letting me make use of many hitherto unpublished papers, letters and documents including their own Minute Books and the Headmaster's annual reports.

Apart from the books mentioned in the notes, I have also drawn on the following:

H.C. Adams, *Wykehamica* (1878)

T.F. Kirby, *Annals of Winchester College* (1892)

A.F. Leach, *A History of Winchester College* (1899)

A.K. Cook, *About Winchester College* (1917)

J.D'E. Firth, *Winchester College* (1949)

Report of Her Majesty's Commissioners appointed to inquire into the Revenues and Management of certain Colleges and Schools and the studies pursued and the Instruction given therein (1864)

The Public Schools and the General Educational System (HMSO, 1944)

The Public Schools Commission (HMSO, 1968)

T.F. Kirby, *Winchester Scholars* (1888)

Winchester College Register 1836-1906 (ed. J.B. Wainewright 1907); 1867-1920 (ed. H.J. Hardy 1923); 1884-1934 (ed. M.S. Leigh 1940); 1901-1945 (edd. E.R. Wilson and H.A. Jackson 1956); 1915-1960 (ed. L.H. Lamb 1974)

A large number of memoirs, including these Winchester pamphlets

J.S. Furley, *Winchester in 1867* (u.d.)

(G.H. Blore), *College in the Eighties* (1947)

(A.L. Irvine), *College in the Nineties* (1947)

(A.N. Palmer), *Winchester 1900-1905* (1954)

Spencer Leeson, *College 1901 to 1911* (1956)

CHAPTER I

Page 1, para.1, page 2 para.3

The text of the Latin is given in Appendices to Kirby's *Annals*. However his transcription is not always reliable, and I am grateful to Roger Custance for pointing out to me an error which makes nonsense of the translation of the Charter by Leach *op.cit.*p.65.

Page 1 para.2

For the early history of New College, see J. Buxton and P. Williams: *New College* (1979) ch.I, V.

Page 6 para.2

The Fiennes legend is explored in Leach p.339 ff.

Page 6 para.3

The papers of Warden Bigg are listed in W.C.M. p.41. See also Cook *op.cit.*p.218.

Page 8 para.2

Biographical works on Winchester Headmasters include:

> C.A.E. Moberly: *Dulce Domum, Bishop Moberly and his Friends* (1911)
>
> Lady Laura Ridding: *George Ridding, Schoolmaster and Bishop* (1908)
>
> Lord Charnwood: *Discourses and Letters of Bishop Burge* (1930)
>
> J.D'E. Firth: *Rendall of Winchester* (1954)
>
> C.H.G. Hopkins: *Bishop A.T.P. Williams* (1975)
>
> *Spencer Leeson, a Memoir by his Friends* (1958)

CHAPTER II

Page 13 para.1

In addition to the official guides, see for information about the buildings, *Winchester College: its History, Buildings and Customs* by Winchester College Archaeological Society (1926); also the essay by J.H. Harvey in *Winchester College Sixth Centenary Essays* ed. Roger Custance (1982)

Page 14 para.2

For a straightforward account of the development of the Commoner buildings, see the author's article in T.S. no. 27 pp.3-9 (June 1969). Also *Winchester College 1393-1893* by Old Wykehamists (1893), p.112 ff., and E.G. Box *Commoners in My Time 1868-71* (u.d.)

Page 19 para.1

The extraordinary story of the Chapel Glass and its vicissitudes after being removed for cleaning by Messrs. Betton and Evans is best studied in J.H. Harvey: *Winchester College Stained Glass* (1972), with articles by W.F. Oakeshott in T.S. no.4 p.4 (May 1957), and by the author in T.S.

no.33 p.2 (June 1972); see also Kenneth Clark: *Another Part of the Wood* (1974) p.60.

Page 23 para.2 Page 24 para.1

The Odyssey of Warden Nicholas' panelling is described in T.S. no.11 pp.2-4 (June 1961).

Page 26 para.4

The 1956 Appeal was also the occasion for launching *The Trusty Servant*, and the progress of the fund-raising and building programme can be followed in its pages.

CHAPTER III

Page 31 para.1

The Statutes of the College were printed in 1855 (Latin only) at the request of the University Commissioners. A paraphrase in English may be found in Ch. 5 of Kirby's *Annals*, where the Latin is also printed as Appendix XI. In 1984 the author translated them in full for the Warden and Fellows.

Page 39 para.3

The story of the identifying of the Malory manuscript is told by Walter Oakeshott in T.S. no. 41 p.3 ff. (June 1976).

Page 40 para.5

The quotation about Fearon's teaching comes from G.H. Blore *op.cit.* p.37. On Rendall and Williams I am particularly indebted to C.G. Stevens' unpublished *Winton*, Vol. 4.

Page 41 para. 2

There is a considerable file of *Mushriana* in the Wiccamica Collection. The editions of the Dictionary call themselves the 5th edition (1880), 6th (1888), and 7th (revised and enlarged, 1901).

Page 44 para.3

In this account of the Tunding Row I owe much to Peter Gwyn who allowed me to read in manuscript and make use of the essay on George Ridding that he has contributed to *Winchester College Sixth Centenary Essays.*

Page 48 para.3, Page 50 para.2

Desmond Lee's speech is reported in T.S. no. 16 p.3 (Dec.1963). John Thorn's sermon on "an informed compassion" is printed in W. 1173 p.274 (1968); his article on modern dullness is in T.S. no.46 p.2 (Nov.1978).

Page 51 para.2

On the psychological effects of boarding, see e.g. Royston Lambert: *The Hothouse Society* (1968), and the essay by Anthony Storr (*The Individual and the Group*) in George Macdonald Fraser: *The World of the Public School* (1977).

CHAPTER IV

Page 53 para.2

The account of Election by nomination is from W. Tuckwell, *The Ancient Ways* (1893); see also W.A. Fearon, *The Passing of Old Winchester* (1924) ch.1.

Page 62 para.5

Stories of the incompetence of the first Modern Language teachers are gleefully recounted by a number of witnesses; see e.g. Tuckwell *op.cit.* p.101, Leach pp.465-7.

Page 67 para.4

On Science teaching, see J.M. Gregory: *Winchester College Science School 1904-1979* (1979), Moberly's evidence to the Clarendon Commission para 930-965, 1291-1305, and references in many of the Winchester pamphlets.

CHAPTER V

Page 75 para.1

For the study of religious attitudes at Winchester, see particularly:

> G. Moberly: *Sermons* (1844 and 1848)
> G. Moberly: *A Lecture read in Sixth Chamber to the College Prefects* (1845)
> W.A. Fearon: *Sunday Mornings at Winchester* (1901)
> W.A. Fearon: *The Passing of Old Winchester* p.74 ff.
> J.T. Bramston: *Sermons to Boys* (1890)
> S. Leeson: *Christian Education* (1947)
> J.D'E. Firth: *Towards Renewal* (1950)
> J.D'E. Firth: *The Church and the Schools* (1951)
> *The Wykehamist:* many editorials, articles and letters published between 1963 and 1972.
> P.S. Bates: *Chapel Today* in W. 1239 p. 479 (1975).
> P.S. Bates: *A Faith to Live By* in T.S. no.48 p.4 (Dec. 1979) and correspondence published in the subsequent number.

Page 80 para.2

The account of Arnold's religious ideas given here follows A. Percival: *Very Superior Men* (1973) pp.116-8.

Page 83 para.2

Fearon's sermon was delivered on 26 March 1887, on the 500th anniversary of the laying of the Foundation stone.

Page 83 para.3

I am most grateful to William Heinemann Ltd. for permission to quote this extract from J.F. Toye: *For What We Have Received* (1950) pp.30-31.

Page 89 para. 3

The three surveys of religious opinion were published in *The Wykehamist* as follows: W.1133 p.354 (1964), W.1186 p.438 (1969), W.1274 p.286 (1979).

CHAPTER VI

Page 91 para. 1

On Public School attitudes to games in the 19th century, see J.R. de S. Honey: *Tom Brown's Universe* (1977), pp.104-117.

Brian Simon and Ian Bradley: *The Victorian Public School* (1975) chapters 7,9,10.

Jonathan Gathorne-Hardy: *The Public School Phenomenon* (1977) pp.146-156.

Most of the information in the rest of this chapter comes from the pages of *The Wykehamist*, where for the best part of a century sport tended to be the dominant topic.

Page 94 para. 2

On cricket, see

E.B. Noel: *Winchester College Cricket* (1926)

E.H. Fellowes: *A History of Winchester Cricket* (1930) (with supplement, 1942)

Page 105 para. 3

The early history of Winchester Football has never been fully chronicled, although there are brief descriptions in A. K. Cook: *Hills, Meads and Games* printed in the fifth centenary volume *Winchester College 1393-1893,* and by H. A. Jackson in *Fifty Years of Sport – Eton, Harrow and Winchester* (1922) and *The Oxford Companion to Sports and Games* 1975. These I have supplemented from the word-books of Gordon (1842) and Elmhirst (1843), and from reminiscences in *The Wykehamist*.

Page 110 para. 3

The excerpt from Mallory's letter is quoted in David Robertson: *George Mallory*, published by Faber and Faber (1969) p.107.

CHAPTER VII

Page 116 para. 5

Alan Rannie: *The Story of Music at Winchester College 1394-1969* (1970). On the early history of the Quiristers see Patricia Hooper: *William Whiting* (1978).

Page 120 para. 1

I am most grateful to William Heinemann Ltd. for permission to quote this extract from J.F. Toye: *For What We have Received* (1950) p.27.

Page 126 para.1

I am most grateful to John Murray (Publishers) Ltd. for permission to quote this extract from Kenneth Clark: *Another Part of the Wood* (1974) p.56.

Page 126 para.3

The extract from J.D'E. Firth: *Rendall of Winchester* (1954) p.55 is quoted by kind permission of Oxford University Press.

Page 131 para.2

The story of the Printing Society is told in two articles in *The Wykehamist:* W.1256 p.65 (1977) and W.1260 p.110. The two books produced by Printing Society were: *Fables from Aesop* (1976) and *Cathedrals* (1979).

Page 132 para.3

The early history of Natural History Society is recorded in the Society's report for 1907-9, pp.87-103 — the report of a lecture by C. Griffith, one of the founder members.

Page 134 para.2

G.M.A. Hewett's pamphlet on *Bug-hunting* is undated (?1890's); *The Open-Air Boy* was first published in 1901, and reprinted in 1928.

Page 136 para.1

The books by the Winchester College Archaeological Society are
Winchester: its History, Buildings and People (1914, 3rd edn. 1933)
and
Winchester College: its History, Buildings and Customs (1926).

Page 136 para.1

The St. Catherine's Hill excavation was written up by J.N.L. Myres, C.F.C. Hawkes and C.G. Stevens in the 1931 volume of the proceedings of the Hampshire Field Club.

Page 136 para.2

Early papers of the Shakespeare Society are printed in C.H. Hawkins: *Noctes Shakesperianae* (1887), whose preface also contains a brief account of the society's formation.

Page 136 para.2

For the first theatricals, see R.B. Mansfield: *School Life at Winchester College* (1866) pp.73-6.

CHAPTER VIII

Page 144 para.4

Almost all the information in this chapter comes from the numerous manuscript word-books in the Wiccamica Collection, the earliest by R. Gordon (1842), the latest by C.G. Stevens (completed in 1969). Printed works include: R.G.K. Wrench, *Winchester Word Book*(1891, 2nd edn. 1901) and *Winchester College Notions* by Three Beetleites (1901, 2nd edn. in two volumes 1910). H.J. Wickham was known as the Beetle and the three authors from his old house were J.F.R. Hope, A.H.S. Cripps, and W.H. Lawson.

Page 154 para.2

Ad Portas: see Peter Gwyn's article in W.1189 p.474-6 (1970). Medal Speaking: see Herbert Chitty, *Medal Speaking at Winchester College 1761-1815* (1905).

Page 158 para.1

More about the origins of *Domum* is set out in Appendix 2.

Page 158 para.2

Ridding's sermon on *True Sons* was delivered on 27 September 1873.

CHAPTER IX

Page 162 para.3

Mayors: Morshead 1873, 1876; also Kirby 1887 (he was actually Bursar and not strictly a member of the staff though intellectually well qualified to be so). Fort 1903, Furley 1910, Pinsent 1936.

Page 162 para.4

Jolliphant: "He's a pleasant old stick and the only man I know who still wears a straw hat." (Penguin edn. p.102).

Page 165 para.1

The early years of the London Mission are described in annual reports for *The Wykehamist* (1876 onwards).

Page 165 para.3

Dolling tells his own story in *Ten Years in a Portsmouth Slum* (1896); an appendix contains the letters exchanged between himself and Bishop Davidson over the offending altar.

Page 167 para.1

The Bishop's letter is printed in W.1073 p.230 (1959).

Page 169 para.2

The history of the C.C.F. is contained in J.W. Parr, *The Winchester College Corps* (1957). I thank Messrs. P. and G. Wells for permission to quote from it.

Page 170 para.3

From the *Ad Portas* address by Lord Carver, W.1247 p.564 (1976).

CHAPTER X

Page 177 para.1

The description of Paul Sender comes from *The Living Daylights* © Ian Fleming 1962. *The Living Daylights* is published by Jonathan Cape

Limited and Triad Panther in the book *Octopussy* by Ian Fleming. I am grateful to the Executors of the Fleming Estate for permission to use this quotation.

Page 177 para.2

There have been six articles in *The Trusty Servant* on Wykehamists in fiction: T.S. nos. 14-17 (1962-4) by Ronald Hamilton, and T.S. no.45 (1979) and no.59 (1985) by the author.

Page 178 para.2

Wykehamist careers: T.J.H. Bishop and R.H. Wilkinson, *Winchester and the Public School Elite* (1967).

Page 179 para.1

Wykehamist politicians: Labour (1945) — Pritt, Cripps, Crossman, K. Younger, Gaitskell; Conservative Cabinet (1979) — Whitelaw, Howe, G. Younger, cf.T.S. no.48 p.9 (December 1979).

Page 182 para.1

Wykehamist generals (1980): J.M. Gow, Hugh Beach.

Page 182 para.2

On Frank Thompson, see Freeman Dyson, *Disturbing the Universe* (1979) ch.4 with Bibliography on p.265.

Page 182 para.4 Page 186 para.1, 2

Editor of *The Times:* G.E. Buckle. Novelists: A. Trollope (briefly), N. Monsarrat (reluctantly). Musicians in 1948: S. Wilson (BBC), J. Robertson (opera), G. Warrack (ballet). Actors: Carleton Hobbs, Peter Bull.

Page 186 para.3

In 1966 there were 16 Wykehamist F.R.S. living (St. Paul's was the next school with 10). The Nobel Prize winner was R. L. M. Synge, Chemistry 1952 (jointly).

Page 187 para.4

Winchester intellectuals: contrast the closing words of J. D'E. Firth's address to Dons Common Room 19 Sept 1957, delivered two days before his death and printed in *Budge A Memoir* ed. Ronald Hamilton (1960) p.211, with Lord Vaisey's essay in George Macdonald Fraser, *The World of the Public School* 1977) p.192.

Page 190 para.2

Everest mountaineers (1921): G. H. L. Mallory, G. H. Bullock, H. T. Morshead. Edmund Backhouse's extraordinary story is told in H. Trevor-Roper: *A Hidden Life* 1976).

INDEX